# THE LITTLE BOOK

BY TONYA GILCHRIST

This is the first book in The Little Book Series—a collection of practical guides for educators, leaders, and teams committed to creating conditions where people can think, contribute, and grow.

Each book explores one essential element of human-centered learning and leadership through the Tiny Shifts Framework: research-informed insights paired with immediately actionable moves that transform how we work, lead, and learn together.

## BOOKS IN THE SERIES:

*The Little Book of Agency* (2026)

*Tiny Shifts That Transform How We Learn, Lead, and Grow*

*The Little Book of Inquiry* (2027)

*Tiny Shifts That Transform How We Question, Listen, and Discover*

*The Little Book of Feedback* (2028)

*Tiny Shifts That Transform How We Reflect, Respond, and Refine*

To be notified when new titles are released:

www.tonyagilchrist.com/books

# THE LITTLE BOOK OF AGENCY

## TINY SHIFTS THAT TRANSFORM HOW WE LEARN, LEAD, AND GROW

THE LITTLE BOOK SERIES
BOOK 1

TONYA GILCHRIST

TINY SHIFTS PRESS

Published by Tiny Shifts Press

Sarasota, Florida



Cover design by Tonya Gilchrist

ISBN 979-8-9952538-1-5 (paperback)

First Edition

Printed in the United States of America

The ideas and strategies in this book are drawn from two decades of work with schools, nonprofits, and organizations worldwide. Readers are encouraged to adapt these frameworks thoughtfully to their own contexts.

For speaking inquiries, workshops, and resources: www.tonyagilchrist.com

*To my dad, who understood that love means making space—*
*not filling it.*

*And to everyone who tends the small, quiet work of creating conditions where*
*others can grow—*
*even when no one's watching,*
*even when it's slow,*
*even when the systems resist.*

*Your work matters.*

# CONTENTS

# AUTHOR'S NOTE

## We Are Born with Agency

Agency is not something we give people. It is not a reward. It is not a leadership strategy. It is not a personality trait we either have or don't.

We are *born* with agency—the capacity to act, to influence, to shape.

But agency is like a muscle. It grows when it is exercised. It weakens when it is constrained.

In many of our institutions, people are not short on agency. They are short on *conditions that allow them to use it.*

When systems over-direct, over-measure, and over-control, agency does not disappear. *It turns inward.* It becomes disengagement. It becomes quiet compliance. It becomes burnout.

This book is not about "giving people agency." It is about designing environments where agency can be exercised—consistently, safely, and productively.

Tiny shifts. Real conditions. Lasting impact.

---

This book began with a pattern I couldn't unsee.

A third-grade teacher in Dubai, exhausted from doing brilliant work that felt impossible to sustain.

A leadership team in Singapore, drowning in initiatives they'd never been asked to shape.

A product manager in London, burning out from carrying thinking for a team that had stopped offering ideas.

Different contexts. Different industries. Same quiet frustration.

Everywhere I went—from international schools in Asia to corporate learning teams in Europe to nonprofit organizations in North America—I kept meeting people carrying the same weight:

They wanted to do meaningful work. They cared deeply. But the systems around them were designed for control, *not contribution*.

Teachers who wanted students to think more deeply but felt boxed in by pacing guides and pressures they didn't design. Leaders who wanted teams to take ownership but felt responsible for every single outcome. Coaches and facilitators who believed in growth but found themselves slipping into fixing, rescuing, or over-directing.

Does this sound familiar?

If so, you're not alone. And more importantly: *you're not failing.*

What you're experiencing is a tension that shows up everywhere, across contexts, roles, and sectors:

---

**We say we want agency. But we keep building systems that depend on control.**

---

This book is not an argument against structure, accountability, or leadership. It's an invitation to rethink how those things work together

—and to examine the tiny moves that either open space for agency or quietly shut it down.

## What I've Learned (and What I'm Still Learning)

I've spent my career moving between research and practice—between what we know about learning, motivation, and human development, and what it actually feels like to work inside real systems with real constraints.

I've worked with early years teachers and secondary students, school leaders and district teams, nonprofit organizations and corporate learning departments. The language changes across these contexts. The jargon shifts. But the human patterns underneath? Those rarely do.

People don't resist responsibility because they're unmotivated. They resist it because the conditions don't make it safe—or meaningful—to step forward.

Research on human motivation consistently shows that people are most engaged when they have autonomy, a sense of purpose, and opportunities to develop mastery.[1] These aren't "nice-to-haves"—they're psychological needs. When systems ignore these needs and rely instead on compliance and control, motivation withers. Agency becomes something people want but can't access.

Agency, as I use the word here, is *not* about independence or going it alone. It's about people having the clarity, trust, and support to think, choose, contribute, and grow *with others*. It's relational. It's contextual. And it's deeply shaped by design.

That's why this book focuses on ***tiny shifts.***

Not sweeping reforms.

Not silver bullets.

Not "ten easy steps."

Just small, intentional changes in how we design learning, lead

1. Pink, D.H. (2009). *Drive: The Surprising Truth About What Motivates Us.* Riverhead Books. Pink synthesizes decades of research on intrinsic motivation, showing that autonomy, mastery, and purpose are fundamental to engagement and performance.

teams, ask questions, give feedback, structure time, and share power. Moves that are realistic inside the complexity of real work. Moves that compound over time.

## What You Won't Find Here

You won't find rigid frameworks in this book. You won't find scripts or mandates. What you *will* find are ideas meant to be adapted—not adopted wholesale—and examples drawn from classrooms, organizations, and leadership spaces alike.

I've intentionally written across sectors because the human dynamics underneath learning and work are far more similar than we often admit. A third-grader waiting for permission to revise her writing and a team member waiting for approval to try a new approach? They're experiencing the same thing: uncertainty about whether their thinking matters.

This is also not a book meant to be read once and shelved.

It's a book to return to:

- Before a meeting you're dreading.
- After a lesson that didn't land the way you hoped.
- During a season when control feels tempting and trust feels risky.
- When you need a reminder that you're not alone in this work.

If something here feels uncomfortable at times, that's not a failure of the writing or the reader. Growth usually asks us to loosen our grip before it offers something better in return.

## How to Use This Book

### If you're a classroom teacher:

You might start with Chapters 2, 7, 8, and 9—they're full of daily moves you can try tomorrow.

### If you're a school leader or administrator:

Chapters 1, 12, 13, and 15 might speak most directly to your role, though the daily moves matter for you too.

### If you're in corporate L&D or organizational learning:

Chapters 3, 6, 11, and 14 offer frameworks you can adapt for professional development, leadership programs, and team effectiveness.

### If you're a coach or facilitator:

Chapters 4, 8, 11, and 13 will give you language and tools for the conversations you're already having.

### If you want to read straight through:

Do that! The book builds on itself. But know that you can also jump around based on what your context needs most right now.

## My Hope for You

My hope is that this book feels like a thought partner—one that respects your expertise, honors your context, and nudges you gently toward a different way of seeing and doing the work.

You don't need to change everything. You don't need to become someone else. You just need to decide, again and again, what's worth holding tightly—and what might be better released.

**That's where agency begins.**

Here's to the courage it takes to try something new, the grace we need when it doesn't go perfectly, and the communities that sustain us through it all.

♡ Tonya

# PART ONE
# THE BELIEF SHIFTS
## REFRAMING HOW WE SEE PEOPLE, LEARNING, AND WORK

Here's the uncomfortable truth about agency:

> It doesn't struggle because people don't care. It struggles because the beliefs underneath our systems—beliefs about control, measurement, learning, and success—weren't built to support it.
>
> And in many organizations, these beliefs have created quiet crises:

- Burnout among people doing work that feels increasingly impossible.
- Disengagement masked as professional compliance—people showing up, doing the tasks, but no longer bringing their best thinking.
- Performative empowerment—leaders who say they want ownership while maintaining control over every decision that matters.
- Over-measurement of the things that are easy to count, at the expense of the things that actually matter.

These aren't education problems or corporate problems. They're design problems.

This section is about pulling those beliefs into the light. Not to judge them. Not to shame anyone for holding them. But to ask, honestly:

*Are these beliefs serving us—and are they creating the conditions we actually want?*

Each chapter invites you to try on a different lens. To notice what shifts when you see agency not as independence, but as interdependence. When you see engagement not as compliance, but as thinking. When you measure what you value instead of valuing what's easy to measure.

These aren't just philosophical ideas. They're the foundation everything else builds on. Because once these beliefs shift—even slightly—the daily moves in Part II become not just possible, but obvious.

Let's begin.

# CHAPTER 1

## AGENCY ISN'T INDEPENDENCE —IT'S INTERDEPENDENCE

### Opening Scene

Three moments. Three contexts. Same question.

A fourth-grader finishes a writing draft, walks to the teacher's desk, and asks: "Am I done?"

A product designer wraps up initial concepts for a new feature, emails their manager, and waits: "Is this what you wanted?"

A nonprofit program coordinator completes a community needs assessment, submits the report, and wonders: "Did I do this right?"

---

Different settings. Different work. Same underlying dynamic.

In each case, someone capable is asking permission to stop thinking. Not because they lack skill. Not because they don't care. But because somewhere along the way, they learned that the real measure of success is whether they've satisfied someone else's expectations—not whether they've created something meaningful.

This is what happens when we confuse agency with independence. And independence with going it alone.

---

Let's start with a Grade 4 classroom, because the pattern shows up most clearly there. But as you read, notice: this isn't just about kids. It's about all of us.

It's the last ten minutes of a Grade 4 Writers' Workshop. Students are scattered around the room—some at tables, some on floor cushions, a few tucked into the reading corner. Notebooks are open. Pencils are moving. The room hums with that particular kind of productive energy that comes when everyone is genuinely working.

Amir finishes a sentence, reads it over, then marches up to the teacher's desk, notebook in hand.

"Am I done?" he asks.

Ms. Chen glances at his work, then up at the success criteria chart they co-created last week. It's posted on the wall where everyone can see it: clear, visual, student-friendly.

"Did you check your piece against what we're working toward?" she asks, gesturing toward the chart.

Amir glances at the wall. Shrugs. "Yeah … I think so."

He looks back at her, waiting. "But am I *done*?"

Sound familiar?

If you've spent more than about twelve minutes in a classroom—or a meeting room, or leading a team—you've met an Amir.

---

Now, let's shift the scene.

It's the last ten minutes of a project meeting in a mid-sized tech company. The team has spent the past hour brainstorming ideas for a new customer onboarding flow. The digital whiteboard is covered with sticky notes. The shared doc on the screen is full of half-formed sentences and competing priorities.

Everyone has contributed *something*. But as the meeting winds down, the energy shifts. People start glancing at the project lead.

Finally, someone says what everyone is thinking: "So … what are we actually doing next?"

The lead—let's call her Jenna—looks around the room. She was hoping the team would take ownership of the decision. Instead, they're waiting for her to decide.

Another team member, trying to be helpful, adds: "Just tell us what you want. We'll make it happen."

---

Different rooms. Different ages. Same pattern.

Lots of activity.

Lots of talent.

Very little agency.

## The Problem We Keep Missing

We often say we want people who can "take ownership," "show initiative," and "lead their own learning." These phrases show up in job postings, strategic plans, and teacher evaluation rubrics.

But the way we structure our classrooms, teams, and systems sends a different message:

> *"You can move ... but only inside the lines I've drawn, and only in the direction I've already decided."*

How does this fit with 'freedom within form'

We mistake independence for the whole story—and end up designing for isolation instead of contribution.

But the kind of agency that actually helps people learn, lead, and grow? That lives in something very different.

**It lives in interdependence.** Here's why this distinction matters more than you might think.

## Why This Matters

When I work with schools and organizations around the world, people often tell me they want "more agency"—for students, teachers, or teams. But when we dig into what that actually means, the picture gets fuzzy.

Sometimes "agency" sounds like "everyone off doing their own thing"—which quietly terrifies people responsible for coherence and outcomes.

Sometimes it sounds like "students / teachers / staff now make all the decisions"—which raises immediate concerns about quality and accountability.

Underneath all of these worries is a hidden belief:

**Agency = independence = less need for me.**

If that's the story we're carrying—even unconsciously—no wonder we accidentally shut it down. We hold on to the plan a bit tighter. We write the learning targets and meeting agendas in more detail. We solve problems quickly so no one gets stuck. We talk about "voice and choice," but only at the edges—safe choices that don't actually affect the direction or quality of the work.

The result?

- **Students** who are compliant, but not truly engaged.
- **Teachers** who follow the initiative of the year, but don't feel safe questioning it.
- **Team members** who execute tasks, but don't feel able to shape the work.
- **Leaders** who are exhausted from carrying all the thinking and decisions alone.

In all of these spaces, we see the same exhaustion: people are tired of being asked to "own" something they don't actually have the power to influence.

We say: "Be independent. Take initiative." But we design experiences where people mostly wait for permission.

## Agency Is Not the Same as Autonomy

Before we turn to the good news, we need to clarify something important: **agency and autonomy are not interchangeable.**

Many organizations have embraced autonomy in recent years. They offer flexible work arrangements, choice in how tasks are completed, and freedom within established boundaries. These are valuable. But they are not the same as agency.

**Here's the difference:**

Autonomy is choice within boundaries someone else designed.
Agency is influence over the boundaries themselves.

Autonomy says, "You can choose how to complete this task."
Agency asks, "How might we shape the task together?"

Autonomy can increase motivation. Agency increases ownership.

When people help shape the work—not just execute it—they are far more likely to *own* the work. This is a subtle but critical distinction.

Many organizations offer autonomy while maintaining tight control over purpose, design, and direction. It feels progressive. But it rarely produces deep commitment.

Agency requires something more fundamental: **shared design.**

This is why you can have a team with high autonomy and low agency. They can choose their schedules, their tools, their methods—but if they have no voice in shaping the direction, the priorities, or the measures of success, ownership remains elusive.

Control produces compliance.
Agency produces commitment.

## Here's the Good News

The problem isn't with the people. It's with the picture.

Agency isn't about walking away from each other and proving we can handle it alone. **Agency is about how we move together.**

Research on collaborative learning, communities of practice, and organizational effectiveness all point to the same insight: people perform better, learn deeper, and sustain growth longer when they work interdependently rather than independently.[1] The myth of the lone genius or the self-sufficient individual doesn't match how humans actually learn and work.

When we shift our view from independence to interdependence, everything changes:

We stop asking: *"How do I get them to take more ownership?"*

And instead ask: *"How do we design relationships, routines, and decisions so that ownership is shared?"*

That subtle shift pulls us out of the lonely myth of independence and into a more honest, hopeful way of working:

**We need each other. Agency grows fastest within a community.**

Think about the moments when you've felt most capable, most motivated, most alive in your work. I'm willing to bet you weren't alone. You were part of something—a team, a partnership, a shared endeavor where:

- Your contributions mattered.
- You could see how your work connected to others' work.
- You had clarity about the direction, even as you had space to make choices within it.
- You trusted the people around you—and they trusted you.

That's interdependence. And that's where agency actually lives.

---

1. See Johnson, D.W. & Johnson, R.T. (1989). *Cooperation and Competition: Theory and Research.* Interaction Book Company; and Wenger, E. (1998). *Communities of Practice: Learning, Meaning, and Identity.* Cambridge University Press.

## The Tiny Shift

Here's the tiny shift at the heart of this chapter:

---

**FROM:** Seeing agency as independence
**TO:** Seeing agency as interdependence

---

**Independence says:** "I shouldn't need help. If I do, I'm failing."

**Interdependence says:** "We're connected. My choices matter to you, and your choices matter to me. We can share direction, information, and responsibility."

Independence focuses on the individual as an isolated unit—the student working alone, the teacher closing their classroom door, the team member completing their task without bothering anyone else.

Interdependence focuses on the *network*—the relationships, routines, and agreements that make choice and contribution possible.

When we see agency as interdependence:

- We design *with* students, not just *for* them.
- We plan learning *with* teachers and teams, not *to* them.
- We share decisions with colleagues instead of carrying them alone or hoarding them at the top.
- We create structures that make collaboration expected, not exceptional.

Agency becomes less about "everyone doing their own thing" and more about:

***"How might we move together in ways that honor each person's voice, strengths, and responsibility?"***

That's where agency lives. Not in isolation, but in connection.

## How to Make This Shift

Let's get practical. How do you actually move from independence to interdependence in your classroom, team, or organization?

Here are five moves to start with. They're small. They're doable. And they compound over time.

### 1. Start Small: Name the "We"

Interdependence starts with what we name out loud.

When you're used to working in systems that celebrate independence—*my* class, *my* project, *my* data, *my* results—you have to intentionally bring "we" back into the room.

You don't have to give a speech about it. You can start with tiny language shifts:

**In a classroom:**

- "We're going to co-figure this out today."
- "Here's what we're trying to learn together."
- "Let's think as a community about what's getting in our way."

**In a team meeting:**

- "Here's the shared outcome we're responsible for."
- "We each hold a piece of this. Let's surface what those pieces are."
- "Before we start, let's be really clear about what we're trying to do *together* here."

**In coaching:**

- "Let's think as partners about what's getting in the way."
- "We're both working on this—what are you noticing that I might be missing?"

Language alone won't change everything. But it does something important: **It signals that leadership, learning, and responsibility are shared spaces.**

*Try this tomorrow:*

Before you launch into directions or dive into content, pause and say: "Let's be really clear about what we're trying to do together here."

Then invite others to help finish the sentence.

You're no longer the only one holding the "why" and the "what." You're already practicing interdependence.

## 2. Make It Visible: Map the Web, Not the Ladder

Most systems are organized like ladders. There's someone "at the top," and information flows down. Decisions get made at higher rungs and implemented at lower ones.

Interdependence asks us to see—and show—the *web* instead.

A web has multiple connection points. Influence moves in many directions. People depend on each other horizontally, not just vertically. And when one strand shifts, others feel it.

Try making the web visible in really simple ways:

**With students:**

- Draw a quick map on chart paper showing who's involved in a project or unit.
- Use arrows to show who students will check in with, who they'll learn from, who they'll teach.
- Ask: "Who else might have important ideas about this?" "Who are we learning alongside?"

**With staff or teams:**

- Sketch out everyone involved in a decision, initiative, or goal.

- Show who depends on whom—and for what.
- Ask: "Where are the bottlenecks?" "Where are the invisible contributions?" "Who else needs to be part of this conversation?"

When people see the web, a few things happen:

- They realize they're not alone.
- They see that their choices matter beyond themselves.
- They can step forward to support others—or ask for support —without feeling like they've failed.

**This is agency in action:** Not rugged individualism, but thoughtful contribution inside a living system.

## 3. Build It Into the Culture: Shared Agreements, Shared Decisions

Interdependence becomes real when we embed it in how we *always* work—not just when we're at our best or when someone reminds us.

Here are three culture-level moves that grow interdependent agency:

**a) Co-create working agreements**

Instead of arriving with the rules of engagement fully formed, invite people to shape them:

- "What do we need from each other to do our best thinking here?"
- "What does support look like in this space?"
- "How will we handle it when things get hard or messy?"

Capture those agreements where everyone can see them. Return to them. Revise them as needed. Actually use them.

You're teaching: **In this community, we build the conditions for learning and work together.**

**b) Share decisions where you can**

Not every decision, but some. And probably more than you think.

Ask yourself: *"Where is there genuine room for others to influence the direction?"*

Then ask them:

- "Here's the outcome we can't change. Within that, where do you want to make choices?"
- "We have three options for how we spend this next hour—what makes the most sense based on what we need right now?"
- "What would make this work better from where you sit?"

When you move even *one* decision from "I decide for you" to "we decide with each other," you shift the gravitational pull of the space.

**c) Normalize asking for and offering help**

In independent cultures, asking for help feels like confessing weakness. In interdependent cultures, asking for help is just part of how good work gets done.

You can model this:

- "I realize I can't see this from every angle. What am I missing?"
- "I need help thinking through this part. Who's willing to partner with me?"
- "I got stuck here—can someone share how they approached it?"

You're showing that agency isn't about having all the answers. It's about being willing to engage, contribute, and connect.

## 4. Design for Transfer of Ownership

One of the most powerful ways to build interdependence is to gradually transfer ownership of processes, decisions, and structures to the people doing the work.

This doesn't mean abandoning people. It means scaffolding them toward more autonomy *within* the shared system.

**In classrooms:**

- Start the year co-creating routines. Mid-year, invite students to evaluate and revise them.
- Begin with teacher-led conferences. Gradually move toward peer conferences and self-assessment.

**In teams:**

- Start a new initiative with clear structure. As people gain competence, invite them to adapt it.
- Begin meetings with tight facilitation. Over time, rotate who facilitates and designs the agenda.

The goal isn't to hand everything over all at once. The goal is to create a culture where **ownership naturally shifts toward the people closest to the work**—because they've been prepared to hold it.

## 5. Protect the Relationships That Make Interdependence Possible

Interdependence doesn't survive in transactional cultures. It thrives in relational ones.

This means:

- **Prioritizing connection over efficiency** when it matters. Sometimes the best use of ten minutes is checking in, not checking off tasks.

- **Building in time to reflect together.** Not just "what did we do?" but "how are we working together? What's strengthening our collaboration? What's getting in the way?"
- **Noticing and naming contributions.** When someone supports another person, when thinking shifts because of dialogue, when collaboration creates something none of you could have done alone—say it out loud.

Interdependent agency is relational work. The relationships have to be tended.

## What This Might Look Like in Practice

Let me show you what this shift from independence to interdependence actually looks like in different contexts.

### In a Grade 2 Classroom

**The old way (independence):**

Ms. Rodriguez wants more "student ownership" during Readers' Workshop. She equates this with students choosing books quietly and working alone while she confers. Students are independent—working separately, mostly silent.

But when she sits down with individual readers, she notices something: many of them are stuck and don't know what to do. They wait passively for her to arrive at their spot. They haven't asked peers for help because that's "off-task."

**The shift (interdependence):**

This year, Ms. Rodriguez makes one small change.

Instead of announcing the day's learning focus herself, she posts three possibilities on the whiteboard:

- Noticing how characters change

- Trying a new strategy when a word is tricky
- Talking about our books with partners

She says: "Here are three directions we could grow as readers today. Let's talk about which one feels most important for us right now—and why."

Students "turn and learn" to discuss in pairs. Then they vote as a class. Today, they choose: "Trying a new strategy when a word is tricky."

Now, the learning is still focused. Ms. Rodriguez is still guiding. But ***the direction is shared.***

Throughout the lesson, she invites students to call out when they try a new strategy. She asks: "Who helped you figure something out today?" She creates structures for students to support each other when they get stuck.

**The result:**

Agency here isn't just little humans reading independently in isolated bubbles. It's a group of learners co-owning what they're working on and how they'll support each other in doing it.

### In a Secondary English Department

**The old way (independence):**

The department head is tired of carrying all the decisions about assessment practices. Teachers are equally tired of "new expectations" arriving fully formed in their inboxes.

Every year, the head announces changes. Teachers nod politely, implement with varying degrees of fidelity, and privately resent not being consulted.

**The shift (interdependence):**

The department head calls a meeting and begins differently.

"Instead of me arriving with a finished plan, I want us to co-design the next phase of our assessment work together. Here's the non-negotiable: we need clearer, more consistent evidence of how students are progressing in their writing. Beyond that, I want us to shape this as a team."

They spend the first twenty minutes doing a simple protocol:

- **Individually:** "What are you noticing about assessment in your classes right now?"
- **In trios:** "Where are students—or families, or we—getting confused or frustrated?"
- **As a whole group:** "What patterns do we see?"

From there, they sketch two to three possible next steps. They discuss trade-offs. They vote on a starting point.

The head doesn't disappear. She still holds responsibility for the department. She still facilitates the process. But the work now lives **in the relationships and conversations of the team**—not just in one person's head or inbox.

**The result:**

The team creates a plan they actually believe in. Implementation is stronger because ownership was shared from the beginning. Teachers feel respected. Students experience more coherence across classrooms.

## In a Nonprofit Program Team

**The old way (independence):**

A small nonprofit is designing a community workshop. In the past, the director has planned the entire agenda alone, made all the decisions, and then handed it to the team: "Here's what we're doing."

The team executes. But they don't feel invested. And often, the workshop misses the mark because the director didn't have full context about what participants actually need.

**The shift (interdependence):**

This time, the director invites two team members who'll be facilitating to a planning session. She says:

"I've brought some constraints: the time we have, the expected outcomes, and what the funder needs to see. Within that, I'd like us to co-design. You're closest to the community relationships—I don't want to do this in isolation."

They sketch together on sticky notes, moving pieces around. They ask: "What would feel respectful and empowering for participants?" They adjust based on each person's perspective and expertise.

The director still carries accountability. But she's no longer *the sole owner* of the design.

**The result:**

Interdependence shows up as shared creativity, shared responsibility, and a workshop experience that's stronger because multiple perspectives shaped it.

## In a Corporate L&D Context

**The old way (independence):**

A leadership development program delivers a fully scripted series of workshops. Participants show up, listen, take notes, and leave. The content is solid. But application is inconsistent. And six months later, most leaders can't remember what they learned.

**The shift (interdependence):**

The facilitators redesign the program to build in interdependence from the start:

- Cohort members co-create norms for how they'll support each other.

- Each session includes time to surface real challenges participants are facing on their teams.
- Peer coaching groups are set up with simple structures for asking for help and offering it.
- Participants commit to trying one new approach and reporting back to the group.

One manager shares midway through: "I thought this program would just tell me what good leadership looks like. Instead, I'm realizing I'm learning how to lead *with* my team, not just *on* my team."

**The result:**

Agency here isn't leaders independently "fixing" their people. It's leaders learning to share direction, power, and learning with their teams.

## In a Coaching Conversation

**The old way (independence):**

A coach sits down with a teacher who's feeling overwhelmed. The coach has ideas. Lots of them. She shares strategies, resources, next steps.

The teacher nods. Takes notes. Leaves feeling ... more overwhelmed.

**The shift (interdependence):**

This time, the coach begins differently:

"Can we map out all the people and pieces connected to this class? Not just what you're carrying, but what lives in the students, the routines, the environment, the wider system?"

Together, they draw a quick web on paper.

The teacher suddenly sees:

- She's holding all communication with families alone—there might be ways to share that.
- Students don't yet have clear roles in supporting each other during work time.
- The learning support teacher and counselor aren't connected to the classroom rhythm in intentional ways.

They don't walk away with a plan for the teacher to work *harder*. They walk away with a plan to work more *interdependently*.

**The result:**

Agency looks like the teacher reclaiming some power—not by doing everything herself, but by reshaping how people around her are involved and connected.

## Common Pitfalls (And How to Avoid Them)

When we try to move from independence to interdependence, a few predictable traps can show up. Here's what to watch for:

### 1. Romanticizing Independence

We still secretly celebrate the people who "do it all" and "don't need help." We praise the teacher who stays until 8 PM. The team member who never asks questions. The student who figures everything out alone.

Culture will always follow what we silently praise.

**What to try instead:** Celebrate collaboration as publicly as you celebrate individual achievement. Name moments when asking for help led to better outcomes. Model it yourself.

### 2. Giving Up Structure Entirely

In an effort to empower others, we sometimes swing to the other extreme: "You all decide everything now. Good luck!"

Without clarity, boundaries, and support, people don't feel trusted—they feel abandoned.

**What to try instead:** Be crystal clear about what's non-negotiable, what's flexible, and where you're available to support. Interdependence doesn't mean no leadership. It means shared leadership within a clear container.

### 3. Keeping the Real Constraints a Secret

When leaders or teachers hold back the non-negotiables—the budget limits, the timeline pressures, the standards requirements—others can't genuinely share in decision-making. They can only decorate the edges.

**What to try instead:** Be transparent about constraints upfront. Then invite others to problem-solve within them. Honesty builds trust. Pretend choice erodes it.

### 4. Confusing "Being Nice" with Being Interdependent

Interdependence isn't just about harmony and agreement. It often involves honest feedback, naming tensions, and renegotiating expectations when things aren't working.

**What to try instead:** Create norms for how you'll handle disagreement and difficulty *before* you need them. Interdependence is strengthened by working through hard things together, not avoiding them.

### 5. Trying to Do It All at Once

Shifting a culture from independence to interdependence is significant work. Trying to flip everything overnight usually leaves everyone exhausted, confused, and longing for the old way.

**What to try instead:** Start with one tiny move. Name the "we" in your next meeting. Map one web. Co-create one agreement. Let it build slowly.

Remember: You don't have to solve all of this at once. You just need to make one small, deliberate move toward naming and designing the "we."

## Tiny Shift: Try This Tomorrow

Choose one upcoming lesson, meeting, or conversation. Before it begins, ask yourself: *"What is the piece of this that we genuinely can co-own?"*

Then, at the very start, say out loud: "Here's what we're here to do. Here's what I'm holding. And here's the part I'd like us to shape together."

Invite input—even if it's for a tiny slice:

- The order of agenda items
- How you'll work together during the session
- What success will feel like
- Which example or problem you'll focus on
- How you'll check for understanding

It doesn't have to be big. What matters is that people experience a real, not pretend, moment of shared agency.

You're teaching: "This isn't just my space. It's *our* space."

That's interdependence beginning to take root.

## Reflection Prompts

Use these for yourself, your team, or with a group you're leading:

1. Where in your current work do you most feel like you're carrying things alone? What might shift if you saw this as a web instead of a ladder?

2. Think about a recent lesson, meeting, or project. Who had real influence on the direction? Who was mostly along for the ride? What might it take to shift that balance?

3. What stories about "good" professionalism or teaching do you carry that might overvalue independence? Where did those stories come from?

4. Where could you invite others into shaping goals, agreements, or decisions—without giving away everything or pretending there are no constraints?

5. What might it look like, this week, to model asking for help as a strength rather than a confession of weakness?

6. If your classroom, team, or organization truly embraced interdependence, what would you see, hear, and feel that's different from today?

## Closing Note

Agency isn't a solo performance. It's something we grow in the spaces between us.

When we stop chasing the illusion of perfect independence and start designing for honest interdependence, a few surprising things happen:

- People feel less alone.
- Responsibility is shared more fairly.
- Courage and creativity start to show up in places they hadn't before.
- Work becomes more sustainable—and often, more joyful.

We don't lose our role as leaders, teachers, or facilitators when we embrace interdependence. We simply stop trying to be the *whole* system.

And as we loosen our grip just enough to invite others in, we discover something both humbling and liberating: **We were never meant to do this alone anyway.**

That's where real agency begins.

# CHAPTER 2

## MISTAKING COMPLIANCE FOR ENGAGEMENT

### Opening Scene

You know that feeling when you walk into a classroom—or a conference room—and everything *looks* perfect?

I had that feeling on a Wednesday morning, observing a Grade 7 humanities class.

Students were seated in neat rows. Notebooks open. Eyes forward. Pencils poised.

The teacher was explaining how to structure a persuasive paragraph. Her explanation was clear. Her examples were strong. Every student was silent. No one interrupted. No one asked a question.

A colleague whispered to me: "Wow. They're so engaged."

But I wasn't so sure.

I watched the kid in the third row copying every word the teacher said—writing fast, but processing nothing. Two students in the back were nodding along in perfect rhythm, eyes glazed, waiting for the signal to move on. One girl was quietly counting how many lines she needed to fill to look busy. Another was watching the clock like it was the only thing keeping him tethered to earth.

The room was quiet.

The room was orderly.
The room looked productive.
But the room was *not* alive.

---

Now shift the scene.

It's a quarterly all-staff meeting at a mid-sized nonprofit. Leadership is presenting new strategic priorities. The slide deck is polished. The data is compelling. The timeline is clear.

Everyone is taking notes. Nodding. Listening "attentively."

A board member leans over to the executive director and says, "This team is really engaged."

But after the meeting ends, I overhear a staff member in the hallway: "Does anyone else feel like we talk a lot about serving the community but never actually get to shape anything?"

Another colleague shrugs. "I just keep my head down. It's easier."

Compliance

---

Different spaces. Different stakes. Same dynamic.

**Quiet ≠ engaged.**
**Nodding ≠ invested.**
**Compliance ≠ agency.**

And yet, in almost every sector—education, nonprofits, government, corporate—we keep confusing them.

We mistake the absence of disruption for the presence of ownership. We mistake following directions for understanding. We mistake politeness for participation.

But engagement—the kind that fuels agency—looks nothing like stillness. It looks like thinking. Wrestling. Contributing. Questioning. Sometimes disagreeing.

It looks like *life* in the room. And life rarely sits perfectly still.

Nancy Kline :)

## Why This Matters

Nearly everywhere I go—whether I'm working with a school in Mumbai, a nonprofit in London, or a corporate L&D team in Dubai—I hear the same thing: "We need more engagement."

I get it. When people seem checked out, it's concerning. It's frustrating. It makes us wonder: *Are we failing? Are they failing?*

But here's what I've noticed: When leaders say "we need more engagement," what they often actually mean is "we need people who *look* engaged." Polite. Attentive. Quiet. Following directions. Completing tasks on time.

I can understand why. These behaviors *feel* productive. They feel respectful. They feel safe.

Here's the uncomfortable truth hiding underneath all of it:

**Compliance isn't engagement. We've been confusing the two for way too long.**

There's a reason this happens: Systems reward compliance. Compliance is predictable. Compliance is neat. Compliance is fast. Compliance makes the people in charge feel … in charge. When we're under pressure—which nearly everyone is—control feels like safety.

So we create environments where:

- Students raise their hands only when they're 100% sure of the answer.
- Teachers check boxes instead of exploring possibilities.
- Staff keep their ideas to themselves because there's already a "right answer" floating in the room.
- Team members attend training sessions but apply nothing because it wasn't theirs to begin with.

People learn the script early:

*If I stay quiet …*
*If I do the task the way they want …*

*If I hit the rubric ...*
*If I don't rock the boat ...*
*I am "engaged."*

But *real* engagement is riskier than that. It means bringing your thinking—not just your compliance. It means participating in shaping direction—not just receiving it. It means offering ideas, testing possibilities, and sometimes disagreeing.

Here's the hidden cost when we confuse compliance for engagement:

- We get performance without purpose.
- We get action without investment.
- We get completion without commitment.

People play the game, but *they don't believe in the work*—and that's the opposite of agency.

## The Tiny Shift

Here's the tiny shift at the heart of this chapter:

---

**FROM:** Interpreting stillness as engagement
**TO:** Interpreting *thinking* as engagement

---

Compliance asks: *"Are they doing what I asked?"*

Engagement asks: *"Are they thinking? Are they making meaning? Are they contributing something real?"*

Compliance focuses on the surface: quiet faces, tidy behaviors, clean deliverables.

Engagement focuses on cognition and connection: What's happening inside the learner? Inside the team? What meaning are people making?

When we make this shift:

- We stop praising students who look the most compliant and start noticing students who are actually grappling with ideas.
- We stop running meetings where everyone nods in polite agreement and start creating meetings where thinking is shared—and sometimes challenged.
- We stop designing professional learning, training, or workshops as delivery events and start designing them as learning experiences.
- We stop treating participation as a performance and start treating it as partnership.

Compliance is passive. Engagement is *alive.*
**Agency can only grow where the thinking *lives.***

## How to Make This Shift

So how do you move from valuing compliance to valuing genuine engagement? Here are five practical moves:

### 1. Redefine "Engagement" Out Loud

If you don't change the definition, the culture stays the same. Try naming what engagement actually looks like in your context:

**In a classroom:**

- "Engagement is your thinking, not your silence."
- "We're looking for ideas, questions, connections—not perfection."
- "I'd rather hear your honest confusion than your polite agreement."

**In a meeting:**

- "Engagement means your voice matters here. We need your perspective to see the full picture."
- "Silent agreement doesn't help us make better decisions."
- "If you disagree, that's valuable information. Please share it."

**In a workshop or coaching session:**

- "Our goal isn't to get through the content. Our goal is to make meaning together."
- "Your thinking—even when it's still forming—is what we need in the room."

When you redefine engagement publicly and consistently, you rewrite the expectations.

People start to understand: *This space values my thinking, not just my behavior.*

## 2. Create Structures Where Thinking Has to Show Up

If the structure only requires compliance, that's all you'll get. Try small structural moves that demand thinking:

**In classrooms:**

- **Turn-and-learn** conversations that require sense-making, not just sharing
- **Protocols** that push beyond surface contributions (e.g. "Say something," "Final word," "Chalk talk")
- **Inquiry questions** instead of instructions
- **Think time** built into lessons before anyone speaks (even 30 seconds can change everything)

**In meetings:**

- **Silent writing** before discussion (3 minutes to capture thinking individually)
- **Round-robin reflections** so ideas don't cluster around the loudest voices
- **Small group problem-solving** before whole-group decisions
- **"What's one thing you're noticing?"** instead of "Any questions?"

The important part is this: **Structure acts as a container for thinking.**

Without structure, only the fastest processors or boldest voices show up. With the right structures, everyone's thinking becomes visible and valued.

## 3. Shift Feedback from Right Answers to Reasoning

When the feedback culture celebrates correctness, people hide their thinking. When it celebrates reasoning, people reveal it.

**In classrooms:**

- "Walk me through your thinking."
- "What's another way someone might see this?"
- "What made you decide to try that strategy?"
- "Where did your thinking shift as you worked?"

**In teams:**

- "What led you to that conclusion?"
- "Where is the data pointing you?"
- "What trade-offs did you consider?"
- "What would you do differently next time—and why?"

**In leadership:**

- "What's the logic behind your recommendation?"
- "What possibilities did you explore but set aside?"
- "Help me understand how you're thinking about this."

When people know their *thinking*—not their perfection—is valued, engagement rises. Mistakes become information instead of failures. Uncertainty becomes curiosity instead of weakness.

## 4. Normalize Cognitive Discomfort

The moment something feels challenging, compliant cultures retreat. Engaged cultures lean in.

Try saying out loud:

- "It makes sense if this feels tricky—that means we're thinking."
- "Discomfort is not a problem; it's a signal that learning is happening."
- "If you're confused, you're in good company. Let's work through it together."
- "The easy stuff doesn't teach us much. This is where growth lives."

In research on learning, we know that productive struggle—the kind where learners are challenged but supported—is essential for deep understanding.[1] But in many cultures, struggle gets interpreted as failure.

**Teach teams and students alike that productive struggle is not a sign of failure—it's a sign of *learning*.**

When you normalize discomfort, people stop hiding when they

1. For more on productive struggle and its role in learning, see Kapur, M. (2016). "Examining Productive Failure, Productive Success, Unproductive Failure, and Unproductive Success in Learning," *Educational Psychologist*, 51(2), 289-299.

don't understand. They start asking questions. They start trying things. They start engaging.

## 5. Invite Genuine Contribution

If you want engagement, people need something *real* to influence. Try moves like:

**In planning:**

- "Here are the constraints. Within that, what would you recommend?"
- "Which part of this process should we redesign together?"
- "What examples would make this most relevant for you?"
- "What's missing from this plan?"

**In implementation:**

- "How would you adapt this to fit your context?"
- "What would you keep? What would you change?"
- "Where do you see opportunities we haven't named yet?"

**In reflection:**

- "What worked that we should protect?"
- "What got in the way that we could remove?"
- "What surprised you?"

When people shape the work—even in small ways—they show up differently. They stop waiting to be told what to do. They start thinking ahead. They start owning outcomes.

That's engagement.

## What This Might Look Like in Practice

Let me show you what this shift from compliance to engagement can actually look like in different contexts.

### In a Grade 3 Classroom

**The situation:**

During math, students were quietly completing word problems. The teacher realized the silence was misleading—students weren't thinking deeply; they were following patterns they'd memorized without understanding.

**The shift:**

She introduced a simple change: "Before you write your answer, talk to a partner about what the problem is actually asking you to figure out."

**What happened:**

Suddenly:

- Questions emerged that had been invisible before
- Misconceptions surfaced early enough to address them
- Students began comparing strategies: "I did it this way, but you did it that way—why?"
- The room got louder, messier, and infinitely more engaged

The teacher told me later: "I thought I wanted quiet. But what I actually wanted was *thinking*—and thinking is rarely silent."

## In a High School Faculty Meeting

**The situation:**

The assistant principal needed to introduce a new approach to grading and assessment. In the past, she'd presented fully formed policies. Teachers would nod politely, then implement inconsistently—or not at all.

**The shift:**

Instead of presenting a new grading policy, she posted three student work samples on the screen and said: "Let's analyze these together. What do you notice? What do you wonder? Where do you disagree with each other?"

**What happened:**

Teachers came alive. They debated. They asked questions. They raised concerns nobody would have voiced if she'd just presented a finished policy.

The assistant principal walked away with:

- A clearer understanding of what teachers actually needed
- Buy-in she never would have gotten through a presentation
- A far more robust plan because it was shaped by the people who would implement it

She told me: "I thought I was saving time by arriving with answers, but I was actually creating more work for myself later when teachers didn't understand or didn't agree."

## In a Nonprofit Team

Use this for SG. mtgs.

**The situation:**

A program director realized her team meetings were filled with polite agreement but lacked real conversation. Decisions got made, but implementation was inconsistent because people weren't actually aligned.

**The shift:**

She brought a new structure to how the team made decisions together:

1. Individuals write down what they believe is the most urgent problem (2 minutes)
2. Small groups compare thinking and look for patterns (5 minutes)
3. Whole group surfaces themes and tensions (10 minutes)
4. Decisions are shaped together based on what emerged (15 minutes)

**What happened:**

Engagement skyrocketed. People were no longer *attending* meetings; they were *participating* in decisions.

One team member said: "For the first time, I felt like my perspective actually mattered. Not just in theory—in practice."

## In a Corporate L&D Program

**The situation:**

A leadership development program had strong content, but participants struggled to apply it. Six months later, most leaders couldn't remember what they'd learned.

**The shift:**

The program designers replaced the final multiple-choice assessment with something new:

"Bring a recent leadership challenge you faced. Walk us through your decision-making. What did you consider? Why? What would you do differently now?"

**What happened:**

Participants were hesitant at first—but then came alive.

Leaders began learning from each other's *thinking,* not just repeating the program's slides. They challenged assumptions. They offered alternative approaches. They connected the content to their real work.

One participant said: "I came in expecting a formula. What I got instead was a way of *seeing*. That's harder to explain—and worth so much more."

## Common Pitfalls (And How to Avoid Them)

### 1. Confusing Participation with Noise

Engagement isn't chaos. It's thinking.

Some of the quietest moments can be the richest—if genuine thinking is happening.

**What to try instead:** Pay attention to what's happening cognitively, not just behaviorally. Are people making meaning? Connecting ideas? Grappling with complexity? That's engagement, whether it's loud or quiet.

## 2. Praising Compliance Too Loudly

Compliments like "You're so well-behaved" or "Thanks for not causing trouble" teach people that invisibility is valued.

**What to try instead:** Notice and name thinking. "I saw you revise your approach when that didn't work." "You asked a question that shifted how we're all seeing this." "Your confusion helped us realize something important."

## 3. Asking for Engagement but Controlling Every Decision

If there's nothing real to contribute to, people retreat to compliance.

**What to try instead:** Create genuine opportunities for influence. Even small choices matter. "Should we tackle this in pairs or small groups?" "Which example should we unpack together?" Give people something real to shape.

## 4. Equating Disagreement with Dysfunction

Engaged cultures tolerate—and expect—differences in thinking. Compliant cultures avoid them.

**What to try instead:** Normalize productive disagreement. "Who sees this differently?" "What are we not considering?" "Where's the tension we need to address?" Tension isn't the problem. Unspoken tension is.

Divergent thought is better with diverse people.

## 5. Trying to Hype People into Engagement

Motivation isn't a performance. It's ownership.

**What to try instead:** Focus on conditions, not cheerleading. Create clarity. Build safety. Invite contribution. Share power where you can. Engagement grows from how work is designed, not how enthusiastically it's pitched.

set the conditions for this to happen.

## Tiny Shift: Try This Tomorrow

Choose an upcoming lesson or meeting. Before it starts, ask yourself: *"What thinking do I hope to see today?"*

Then design one tiny move that makes thinking visible:

- Ask a question with more than one right answer
- Give think time before discussion (at least 30 seconds—yes, time it)
- Invite people to analyze examples or dilemmas instead of listening to a presentation
- Let participants choose which problem, text, or scenario they want to work with
- Ask: "What's one thing here that surprises you?"

Make it small. Make it real.
Make it about thinking, not just behaving.
And watch what happens.

## Reflection Prompts

1. Where in your context do you currently see the highest levels of quiet compliance? What might that be protecting?

2. What signals currently tell people in your space that compliance is the safest choice?

3. When have you mistaken compliance for engagement in the past month? What did you notice when you looked more closely?

4. What structures in your classroom, team, or organization currently reward obedient behavior instead of actual thinking?

5. What one part of your practice—or your team's practice—could shift toward deeper cognitive engagement this week?

6. How do you respond when people disagree or struggle? What message might that send about what you value?

## Closing Note

Compliance may look calm, but it costs us creativity, courage, and connection. Engagement asks more of us—and gives more back.

When we stop being fooled by the polished surface and start paying attention to what's happening underneath, we make space for what matters:

People who think.
People who contribute.
People who bring their full selves to the work.

We don't need rooms full of quiet faces. We need rooms full of *living minds.*

That's how agency grows.

Pad this out w. Nancy Kline!

# CHAPTER 3

## DON'T VALUE WHAT YOU MEASURE —MEASURE WHAT YOU VALUE

### Opening Scene

It's progress-report season at an international school I worked with a few years ago. Teachers are exhausted. Families are confused. The leadership team is knee-deep in color-coded spreadsheets that would make a data analyst weep—not from joy, but from the sheer complexity of it all.

At one meeting, a teacher points at a particularly impressive chart on the screen—multiple tabs, conditional formatting, graphs that update in real-time—and asks the question everyone is secretly wondering:

"So ... what does any of this actually mean for the kids?"

The room goes quiet.

Eventually someone offers the safest possible answer: "Well ... it shows they're progressing."

The teacher waits.

"Progressing toward what? Progressing *how*? In ways that matter to whom?"

No one can quite say.

---

Now shift settings.

A corporate team is preparing for quarterly reviews. Their dashboards are immaculate: conversion rates, pipeline health, engagement percentages, hours logged, response times, tasks completed.

The VP nods approvingly at the screen, then asks: "And what does this tell us about whether the *work* is better than it was last quarter?"

People glance at each other. Someone shifts in their seat. Finally, someone mutters: "Well ... at least it's measurable."

---

Two different rooms. Two different sectors. Same story.

We end up valuing whatever is easiest to measure—even when it's not actually what we care about.

Not because we're careless. Because we're overwhelmed.

And because measuring the right things—authentic learning, thoughtful collaboration, equitable participation, genuine problem-solving—is much harder than counting whatever happens to leave a tidy trail.

The problem *isn't* measurement. The problem is when measurement becomes *the goal* rather than *a window* into the thing we actually value.

This chapter is about pulling those two things apart again.

## Why This Matters

Organizations don't become more strategic by collecting more data. Schools don't become more effective by color-coding more test scores. Teams don't become more aligned by tracking more metrics.

Yet we've all lived inside systems where **measurable = important.**

And so we start shaping behavior around the numbers:

- Students write for the rubric instead of for meaning.

- Employees optimize for metrics that don't reflect their real impact.
- Team members perform for the dashboard instead of the users or families they serve.
- Leaders confuse "visible activity" with "meaningful work."

Over time, people adjust. They get really good at giving us what we measure—even if it's not what we're actually after.

This isn't malicious. It's human. When the stakes are high and the expectations are unclear, people do what feels safest: **they aim for what's being counted.**

We say we value curiosity, collaboration, nuance, creativity, and adaptability. But when the things we actually measure are things like:

- Task completion rates
- Attendance percentages
- Test scores
- Hours logged
- Email response times
- Number of meetings attended
- Velocity or volume

We unintentionally communicate: **"These are the things that count. Everything else is extra."**

That's when compliance masquerades as engagement. That's when initiative dries up. That's when agency withers.

If our measurement systems don't match our values, people will pick measurement every time—because their grade, job security, evaluation, or reputation depends on it. But when we flip the equation—when we measure what we actually care about—we start to see different behaviors, different priorities, and a different sense of purpose.

## The Tiny Shift

Here's the tiny shift at the heart of this chapter:

---

**FROM:** Valuing whatever is easiest to measure
**TO:** Measuring whatever you actually value

---

This shift forces a few essential questions:

- What do we *say* matters here?
- What do our measurement practices *signal* actually matters?
- Where is the gap between those two things?
- And what would happen if our practices aligned with our purpose?

This isn't about abandoning data. It's about reclaiming it as a tool—not a tyrant.

When we measure what we value:

- We create alignment between what we say and what we do
- We make the invisible visible in ways that actually help
- We give people clarity about what matters most
- We free ourselves from optimizing for the wrong things

**Data can illuminate or distort. The choice is in what we choose to count.**

(H) data often distorts.

— Reporting on MH !!!

## How to Make This Shift

### 1. Start With Clarity: Name What You Truly Value

Before you ever design a metric, rubric, dashboard, or checklist, ask the simplest—and often hardest—question: *"What are we really trying to grow here?"*

**For a classroom, it might be:**

- Deeper thinking
- Strategic reading that transfers across texts
- Flexible problem-solving
- Collaborative stamina
- Ownership of learning

**For a nonprofit, it might be:**

- Community empowerment (not just service delivery)
- Relationship quality (not just reach)
- Long-term impact (not just immediate outcomes)

**For a team or organization:**

- Learning agility
- Psychological safety
- Adaptive leadership
- Equitable participation
- Innovation capacity

Your values need to be *lived,* not laminated.

**A quick exercise you can use in any context:**

- List everything you currently measure
- Put a star next to anything that truly aligns with your core purpose
- Circle anything that is easy to measure but not deeply meaningful
- Ask: "What's missing from this list—the things that matter but aren't represented?"

The gaps tell the truth.

## 2. Make It Visible: Design Evidence, Not Surveillance

Evidence doesn't have to be numerical to be meaningful. Here are examples across contexts:

**In classrooms:**

- Audio snippets of student explanations (what they're thinking, not just what they produced)
- Annotated drafts showing decision-making and revision
- Student self-reflections that reveal metacognition
- Quick exit notes about misconceptions, insights, or questions
- Photos of collaborative work in progress

**In teams:**

- Pulse checks that reveal trust, clarity, or alignment (simple 1-5 scales with space for "why")
- Short written reflections about decision-making processes
- Collaborative artifacts (not just individual deliverables)
- Peer feedback on specific behaviors or contributions

**In organizations:**

Children + babies voices

- Stories from stakeholders or clients about moments of impact
- Observations of cross-team collaboration
- Small case studies of real-world problem-solving
- Qualitative data about what's working and what's not, gathered consistently

Qual not just Quant

Evidence becomes richer—and more honest—when it is:

- **Co-constructed** (people help define what counts as evidence)

- **Transparent** (everyone can see it and understand it)
- **Contextual** (it makes sense within the situation)
- **Qualitative + quantitative** (numbers *and* narratives)
- **Connected to actual work** (not separate from the work, but embedded in it)

You're not creating surveillance. You're creating insight.

## 3. Build It Into the Culture: Align Accountability With Purpose

This is where the rubber meets the road.

If what you measure—and reward—doesn't match what you say matters, people will choose the measures every time. They have to. That's how systems work.

To shift this, try three moves:

### a) Reduce the "Shadow Metrics"

Shadow metrics are the ones that aren't officially important but still run the show:

- How many slides you created
- How fast you reply to emails
- How quiet the class is
- How many meetings you attended
- How long you stay after hours
- How polished your draft looks

Bring these into the open. Name them. Ask whether they deserve the power they currently hold. Often, they don't.

### b) Create Measures of What Matters Most

If you value collaboration, measure collaboration—not attendance at meetings.

If you value critical thinking, measure reasoning—not speed.

If you value equity, measure access and inclusion—not just outcomes.

If you value creativity, measure originality—not correctness.

If you value leadership, measure influence—not seniority.

This requires creativity. It's harder than counting tasks. But it's worth it.

**c) Share the Story Behind the Numbers**

A number without a narrative isn't useful.

Invite people to annotate the data with:

- Context: What was happening when this data was collected?
- Insight: What does this tell us? What does it not tell us?
- Decisions: What did we try based on this information?
- Obstacles: What got in the way?
- Next steps: What will we do differently?

That's where agency and ownership actually grow—not in the number itself, but in the meaning people make from it.

## What This Might Look Like in Practice

### In an Elementary Classroom

**The situation:**

A teacher wants to understand her students' reading progress. In the past, she relied solely on running records and reading levels—clean, quantifiable, easy to track.

But she noticed something troubling: the numbers didn't tell her *how* students were thinking as readers.

**The shift:**

She keeps the running records (they have value), but she adds:

- "Can you show me where the text surprised you?"
- "Where did you change your mind about what might happen?"
- "What strategy did you try when you got stuck—and did it work?"

She collects audio clips of these conversations. She keeps sticky notes where students capture their thinking. She asks students to mark places in their books where they noticed themselves growing as readers.

**The result:**

The evidence now shows not just *what* they can read, but *how* they're thinking. The metric becomes the meaning, not just the number.

One student told her: "I used to think reading was about getting to the end. Now I know it's about thinking while I read."

That's evidence of something that matters.

### In a Secondary Math Department

**The situation:**

The department team was frustrated that their assessments mostly rewarded students who worked quickly and quietly. Thoughtful students who took their time were penalized. Students who showed creative approaches but made calculation errors got low scores.

**The shift:**

They co-designed a new structure:

- Each assessment includes at least one reasoning task where students must explain their thinking
- Students annotate their work to show their decision-making process
- Brief reflections accompany final answers: "What strategy did you use and why?"
- Partial credit is given for sound reasoning even if the final answer is incorrect

**The result:**

Suddenly:

- Quiet students' thinking became visible
- High-achieving students had to demonstrate understanding, not just speed
- Teachers could see misconceptions they'd never noticed before
- Students started valuing their thinking process, not just their answers

One teacher said: "We didn't add more tests. We added more *truth*."

## In a Corporate Team

**The situation:**

A manager noticed her team was optimizing for output: number of tasks completed, number of tickets closed, number of hours logged.

But the work they actually valued—innovation, user impact, sustainable solutions—wasn't being measured at all.

**The shift:**

She changed their team metrics:

- Each sprint includes one "value story": a concrete example of a user helped, problem solved, or improvement made
- Team members rate their sense of clarity and collaboration weekly (1-5 scale) and discuss dips
- Success is defined by impact milestones, not task counts
- Retros focus on "What did we learn?" not just "What did we ship?"

**The result:**

People began solving the real problems again—not just the measurable ones.

One team member said: "I used to feel like a task-completion machine. Now I feel like I'm contributing to something worth doing."

### In a Nonprofit Organization

**The situation:**

A youth-serving nonprofit used to measure only attendance and number of workshops delivered.

But what they actually valued was connection, empowerment, and youth leadership development. None of that was captured in their reports.

**The shift:**

They began collecting different evidence:

- Stories from youth about moments they felt heard or capable
- Reflections from mentors about changes in young people's confidence
- Quick surveys asking: "What did you contribute today?"
- Observations of peer leadership moments
- Youth-led project documentation

**The result:**

Funding reports became richer. Program design became sharper. The data actually meant something—to staff, to youth, and to funders.

The executive director told me: "We're finally measuring what we've always cared about. And it's changing how we work."

## Common Pitfalls (And How to Avoid Them)

### 1. Mistaking "Hard to Measure" for "Not Important"

Some of the most valuable things—trust, agency, curiosity, creativity—are inherently messy to measure.

That doesn't mean they don't matter. It means we need to get more creative about evidence.

**What to try instead:** Accept that some things require qualitative evidence, observation, or narrative. Not everything fits in a spreadsheet. And that's okay.

### 2. Measuring Everything

If everything is important, nothing is. When measurement sprawls across too many indicators, people lose sight of what actually matters—and energy gets spent tracking things instead of improving them.

**What to try instead:** Prioritize. What are the 2-3 things that matter most right now? Focus your measurement energy there. Let some things remain unmeasured.

### 3. Using Measurement as Judgment Instead of Insight

When data becomes a weapon—used to evaluate, compare, or punish—people shut down. They game the system. They hide struggles.

**What to try instead:** Frame measurement as learning. "What is this telling us?" not "Who is succeeding or failing?"

### 4. Creating Performative Metrics

When data becomes theater—when people are performing for the dashboard rather than working toward the goal—learning dies.

**What to try instead:** Keep asking: "Is this measure changing behavior in ways that align with our values? Or is it creating performance that looks good but doesn't actually matter?"

### 5. Assuming More Data = More Clarity

Often, more data just creates more noise. When people are swimming in metrics, they spend their time managing the data instead of responding to what it reveals—and the most important signals get lost in the volume.

**What to try instead:** Focus on signal, not volume. What's the smallest amount of the most meaningful evidence you could collect?

### 6. Keeping Values Aspirational Instead of Operational

If you don't measure it—in some form—it won't last.

**What to try instead:** If you truly value something, find *some* way to track evidence of it. Even imperfect measurement keeps important things visible.

## Tiny Shift: Try This Tomorrow

Choose one project, lesson, initiative, or team process.

Ask: *"What is the real outcome I want here—the one that matters even if no one ever sees the data?"*

Then identify one small piece of evidence that would help you understand that outcome. Something meaningful, even if it's not perfectly measurable.

Use that tomorrow. Just one piece.

You're not rebuilding your entire measurement system. You're building alignment between what you say you value and what you actually pay attention to.

Over time, that alignment changes everything.

## Reflection Prompts

1. What metrics currently drive your decisions—formally or informally? Which of those truly align with your purpose?

2. What values do you carry that rarely show up in your data?

3. When do you most notice the tension between "what's measurable" and "what's meaningful"?

4. What would be different if your team, classroom, or organization stopped measuring for compliance and started measuring for growth?

5. Where could you add one small piece of evidence that better reflects what you actually care about?

6. Who might you need to involve to ensure that measurement feels shared, fair, and purposeful—not imposed from above?

## Closing Note

Measurement is powerful.

It can illuminate. It can distort.

It can liberate. It can trap.

But when measurement is aligned with what we value—when it's rooted in purpose, not pressure—it becomes a tool for agency, not a barrier to it.

When we measure what matters:

- Learning becomes deeper
- Relationships become stronger
- Work becomes more meaningful
- Decisions become more human

The numbers don't disappear. They just take their rightful place: as one of many ways we understand the story—not the story itself.

# CHAPTER 4

## THE ACTIVE VIEW OF LEARNING

### Opening Scene

A secondary science class is halfway through a lab. Students are measuring temperature changes in chemical reactions. Jotting numbers. Checking timers. Recording observations in their notebooks.

From the doorway, it looks productive. It looks focused. It looks … fine.

The teacher circulates, checking in: "How's it going?"

Students nod.

"Good."

"Fine."

"We're doing it."

But when the teacher pauses beside one pair and asks, "So why is this reaction causing the temperature to rise?" she's met with blank stares.

One student finally offers, unsure: "We're … measuring it?"

The students aren't misbehaving. They're not off-task. They're following the procedure perfectly.

They're compliant—just not learning.

---

Now picture a very different room.

It's a mixed-grade literacy block in an international school. On one side of the classroom, two Grade 4 students are debating whether a character is changing or simply revealing something the reader hadn't noticed before. Their voices overlap, urgent with ideas.

Across the room, a small group revisits a model text, searching for specific craft moves they might borrow for their own writing. They're marking the page with sticky notes, passing the book back and forth.

Nearby, a teacher confers with a student. Both are leaning over a notebook, pencils tapping as they test an idea aloud: "What if you moved this part here? What might that do?"

There's movement. Noise. Thinking.

Not perfect. But *alive.*

---

This is the difference between doing the task and doing the thinking. Between performing moves and making meaning. Between the *appearance* of learning and the *act* of learning.

## Why This Matters

Across schools, organizations, and teams, we often assume learning happens because activity is happening.

Students are quiet. Teachers are busy.

Teams are working through agendas. Slides are projected, notes are taken, deliverables are completed.

But the *Active View of Learning*[1] challenges a comfortable assumption:

---

1. This draws on constructivist learning theory and the work of scholars like Michael Pressley and others who emphasize that learning is an active, strategic process. For more, see Pressley, M. & Harris, K.R. (2006). "Cognitive Strategies Instruction: From Basic Research to Classroom Instruction."

**Learning isn't something that happens TO people. It's something people DO.**

And what matters most isn't whether the task gets done—it's whether the learner is actively connecting ideas, questioning, testing, revising, and making meaning.

When schools or organizations operate from a passive view of learning, a few predictable patterns show up:

- We over-explain instead of letting people wrestle with ideas
- We design lessons where teachers do the heavy cognitive lifting while students watch
- We mistake participation (being present, looking busy) for deep understanding
- We assume "engagement" means people are simply behaving well

This creates two dangerous illusions:

- **The illusion of mastery** (because products look polished)
- **The illusion of progress** (because tasks are completed)

But polished products can hide shallow understanding. Completed tasks don't always mean learning happened.

The *Active View of Learning* replaces illusions with something more honest—and more empowering:

**Learning is the result of purposeful thinking. And thinking thrives when learners are invited into the process, not carried through it.**

## The Tiny Shift

Here's the tiny shift at the heart of this chapter:

**FROM:** Seeing learning as the completion of tasks
**TO:** Seeing learning as the construction of meaning

The *Active View of Learning* reframes three big assumptions:

**Old view:** If learners follow the steps, they'll understand.
**Active view:** If learners think deeply, strategically, and socially, they'll understand.

**Old view:** Teachers / experts hold the knowledge and deliver it.
**Active view:** Teachers / experts design the conditions where learners build knowledge.

**Old view:** Engagement is visible.
**Active view:** Engagement is cognitive.

This shift doesn't reduce the role of teachers, leaders, or facilitators. *It elevates it.* Your job becomes designing thinking, not delivering content.

## Where We Often Get Stuck

Even when we believe in active learning, a few traps pull us back toward passivity:

### 1. Mistaking Busyness for Depth

Highlighters moving across paper doesn't equal understanding. Neither does a flurry of sticky notes, animated group work, or a polished slide deck.

Activity can be a sign of learning, or it can be a sign of compliance dressed up as engagement.

The question is: *What thinking is actually happening?*

## 2. Over-Scaffolding

When we break learning into too many tiny, pre-digested steps, learners never get to sense-make. They just follow instructions.

We think we're helping. We're actually removing the very cognitive work that leads to understanding.

## 3. Fear of Struggle

Teachers and leaders want people to feel successful—so we unintentionally remove productive struggle.

But struggle is where learning lives. When we smooth out every bump, we also smooth out the thinking.

## 4. Over-Reliance on Telling

Explaining is faster. It feels efficient. It gives us the illusion of control.

But it's also the quickest way to ensure learners don't have to think. When we do all the cognitive work for them, they become dependent on us to do it again next time.

## 5. Performance Culture

When polished products matter more than the thinking that created them, we teach compliance, not cognition.

Students learn to produce what looks good. Employees learn to deliver what's expected. But neither develops the capacity to think independently.

These patterns aren't failures. They're habits inherited from systems built on seat time, coverage, and pacing guides.

Changing the system starts with changing the view.

## How to Make This Shift

### 1. Design for Thinking, Not Just Doing

Before planning a lesson, meeting, or session, ask:

> *"What **thinking** do I want people to do here?"*

Not the activity. *The thinking.*
Examples of the kind of thinking you might design for:

- Comparing and contrasting
- Justifying a position
- Evaluating options
- Predicting outcomes
- Connecting to prior knowledge
- Prototyping solutions
- Revising based on feedback
- Applying a concept to a new situation
- Distinguishing between similar ideas

Then build the task around that cognitive work.

### 2. Make the Cognitive Work Explicit

Tell learners the kind of thinking they're practicing.

> "You're not just writing a paragraph. You're evaluating evidence and building an argument."

> "You're not just discussing. You're comparing perspectives and looking for patterns."

> "You're not just solving problems. You're developing a strategy you can use again."

Labeling the thinking lifts it into awareness—and makes *transfer* possible. When students and team members can name the thinking they're doing, they can *use it again* in new contexts.

### 3. Use Models as Thinking Tools, Not Templates

Models should spark questions and analysis, not dictate conformity.

**Instead of:** "Make yours look like this."
**Try:** "What do you notice this writer/designer/problem-solver did that strengthened their work? How might we borrow that move—or adapt it—for our own purposes?"

This shifts models from things to copy into things to learn from.

### 4. Add Productive Struggle—Without Panic

Give space for the wobble.

A good rule of thumb: **If learners can complete the task without thinking, the task needs redesign.**

Productive struggle is discomfort with a purpose. It's the feeling of your brain working hard to make sense of something.

It's *not:* confusion without support.

It *is:* challenge within reach, with scaffolds available.

### 5. Make Thinking Social

Thinking deepens when shared. Structures like partner talk, protocols, conferring, micro-debates, and peer coaching help learners:

- Clarify their own ideas by articulating them
- Test assumptions by hearing other perspectives
- Notice misunderstandings before they harden
- Build on each other's thinking

Learning becomes collective, not a solo performance.

## What This Might Look Like in Practice

### In a Grade 3 Classroom

**The old way:**

The teacher starts a math lesson by demonstrating how to solve word problems. She models step-by-step. Students watch. Then they try similar problems on their own.

Many students can replicate the steps. Fewer understand why those steps work.

**The shift:**

Instead, the teacher asks students to analyze two sample solutions to a word problem—one correct, one with a common error.

"Which solution makes more sense? Why?"
"What mistake do you notice in the other one?"
"What would you revise?"

Students actively engage in comparing, critiquing, and refining strategies—before they ever solve their own problem.

**The result:**

They're thinking like mathematicians, not just following procedures. When they tackle their own problems, they have strategies—and the understanding behind them.

## In a Secondary Humanities Class

**The old way:**

After reading a novel, the teacher hands students a list of themes to track. Students find evidence for the themes the teacher has already identified.

**The shift:**

Instead, small groups generate claims they believe the text is making. They compare their ideas. They argue. They revise based on evidence from passages.

The goal isn't a "right" theme list—it's deep interpretation and the ability to defend a claim.

**The result:**

Students aren't hunting for the teacher's answer. They're constructing meaning. The thinking is theirs.

## In an Upper Primary Reading Classroom

**The strategy:**

A teacher implements reciprocal teaching[2]—a research-informed approach developed by Palincsar and Brown that has decades of evidence showing its effectiveness for reading comprehension.

Students take turns leading small group discussions using four strategies:

---

2. Palincsar, A.S. & Brown, A.L. (1984). "Reciprocal Teaching of Comprehension-Fostering and Comprehension-Monitoring Activities," *Cognition and Instruction*, 1(2), 117-175. Multiple meta-analyses confirm reciprocal teaching's effectiveness across ages and contexts.

- **Predicting:** What might happen next?
- **Questioning:** What's unclear or important?
- **Clarifying:** What needs explanation?
- **Summarizing:** What's the main idea?

**The shift:**

Instead of the teacher asking all the comprehension questions, students generate them. Instead of the teacher summarizing, students practice that thinking. The teacher coaches from the side, not the center.

**The result:**

Reading comprehension improves significantly—not because students are being told what the text means, but because they're actively constructing meaning together. The cognitive work belongs to them.

One student explained: "Before, I just read and hoped I got it. Now I know what to do when I'm confused."

## In an Early Years Setting

**The old way:**

During an inquiry block, the teacher tells students what will happen when two materials mix. Students observe to confirm what she said.

**The shift:**

Instead, the teacher invites children to predict what will happen. She asks:

"What makes you think that?"
"What could we test?"
"What might surprise us?"

After observing, they revisit their predictions: "What was different than you expected? Why do you think that happened?"

**The result:**

The thinking is the curriculum. Children aren't just watching a demonstration—they're doing science.

## In a School Leadership Team

**The old way:**

Leaders arrive at a staff meeting with a fully formed plan for instructional priorities. They present it. Staff listen. The plan gets implemented—with varying degrees of buy-in.

**The shift:**

Instead, leaders invite staff into meaning-making:

"What instructional patterns are we seeing across divisions?"
"What questions do the data raise for you?"
"What's the learning our system needs most right now?"

Leaders still hold direction and responsibility—but the thinking is constructed together.

**The result:**

Staff understand the "why" because they helped build it. Implementation is stronger because ownership is shared.

### In a Corporate L&D Program

**The old way:**

During a leadership workshop, the facilitator presents best practices through slides and lecture. Participants take notes. They leave with information but limited application.

**The shift:**

Instead, participants analyze short case studies of common team challenges.

The facilitator asks:

"What assumptions are driving these decisions?"
"What alternative strategies could strengthen the outcome?"
"What thinking patterns do you notice in yourself as you consider this?"

Leaders aren't taught. Leadership thinking is surfaced, examined, and refined through structured cognitive work.

**The result:**

Participants leave with thinking skills, not just information. They can apply those skills to new situations.

## Common Pitfalls (And How to Avoid Them)

### 1. Turning Active Learning Into Chaos

More thinking doesn't mean less structure. The structure just shifts. Instead of structuring the content delivery, you're structuring the thinking process.

**What to try instead:** Use protocols, clear questions, and time boundaries to keep thinking focused without controlling it.

### 2. Equating "Voice" With Unlimited Choice

Choice must still serve learning. Not all choices are equally valuable.

**What to try instead:** Offer choice within a frame. "We're all working toward this understanding—you get to choose the path, the materials, or the way you'll demonstrate it."

### 3. Assuming Everyone Will Struggle the Same Amount

Different learners need different forms of support—but none should be shielded from thinking.

**What to try instead:** Differentiate the support, *not* the thinking. Everyone gets to grapple with meaningful ideas; some get more scaffolding along the way.

### 4. Using Tasks That Look Collaborative but Are Actually Passive

Group work can be as passive as worksheets if designed poorly. If one person does the thinking while others copy, nothing has changed.

**What to try instead:** Design group tasks where everyone's thinking is required. Use protocols that ensure all voices contribute.

### 5. Returning to Telling When Time Is Tight

Speed is seductive. But it rarely leads to understanding.

**What to try instead:** Protect time for thinking—even when (especially when) you feel rushed. The thinking you skip now will cost you later in reteaching.

## Tiny Shift: Try This Tomorrow

Before your next lesson, session, or meeting, ask: *"What is the one most important piece of thinking I want people to do today?"*

Then say it out loud at the start: "Here's the thinking we're practicing today: [comparing strategies, evaluating options, connecting ideas, etc.]. That's our focus."

Design one small moment where learners must do that thinking—a comparison, a prediction, a justification, a revision.

Keep it tight. Keep it simple. Keep it cognitive.

It will change the energy in the room immediately.

## Reflection Prompts

1. Where in your current practice do people complete tasks without doing much thinking? What might that be costing you—and them?

2. When have you confused visible engagement (busyness, activity) with cognitive engagement (thinking, meaning-making)?

3. Which kinds of thinking show up most often in your space? Which are missing?

4. What's one routine you could redesign to invite deeper meaning-making instead of task completion?

5. When in the past week did learners (students or adults) do genuine thinking? What made that moment possible? What conditions supported it?

6. Where are you currently doing the cognitive work that learners could—and should—be doing themselves?

## Closing Note

When you embrace an *Active View of Learning*, you stop asking:

> *"How do I get them to pay attention?"*
> *"How do I keep them engaged?"*

And you start asking:

*"What thinking lives at the heart of this work?"*
*"How do I design so learners get to do that thinking?"*

People don't become independent by being carried. They become independent by thinking. And thinking grows best in spaces where it's intentionally designed, named, shared, and valued.

**This is where real learning—and real agency—begins.**

# CHAPTER 5

## THE POWER OF SHARED DIRECTION

### Opening Scene

A Grade 4 team gathers around a table covered in planners, sticky notes, curriculum documents, and half-finished coffee cups.

They're preparing for an inquiry unit on the concept of systems—with ecosystems as the primary focus. Everyone cares. Everyone works hard. Everyone showed up prepared.

But as soon as planning begins, the energy shifts.

One teacher wants to emphasize hands-on experiments. Another wants more explicit vocabulary instruction. A third is concerned about time and suggests cutting the culminating project. A fourth wants students to design their own investigations from start to finish.

All are good ideas.

All are grounded in solid pedagogy.

None point in the same direction.

By the end of the meeting, they settle on a compromise—not because it's the strongest plan, but because they're out of time and need to move forward. They walk away with a loosely aligned unit and a collective sigh that says: *This is good enough.*

---

Meanwhile, across the world, a product development team at a mid-sized tech company faces a remarkably similar challenge.

They're designing a new client onboarding process.

The product lead believes the focus should be speed—get clients up and running fast. The UX specialist argues for seamlessness—reduce friction at every step. The marketing director wants personalization—make every client feel seen. The client success manager insists on consistency—everyone should have the same high-quality experience.

Again, every idea has merit.

Again, the team leaves the meeting feeling scattered, unclear about which priority should actually drive their decisions.

---

Two different sectors. Two thoughtful teams. Same problem.

It's hard to build momentum when the compass keeps shifting. Clarity isn't a luxury—it's a necessity for progress, coherence, and psychological safety.

## Why This Matters

Humans do better work—and deeper learning—when they know where they're headed and why it matters.

**Shared direction creates:**

- **Focus** (what we're doing)
- **Coherence** (why it matters)
- **Confidence** (how we'll get there)
- **Commitment** (we're in this together)

Without it, even the most skilled teams spin their wheels. They confuse motion with progress. They work hard but not necessarily in alignment. They unintentionally design inconsistent experiences for learners, clients, or stakeholders.

**In schools, lack of shared direction shows up as:**

- Classrooms pulling in different instructional directions (students experience whiplash moving between teachers)
- Team agreements that sit in binders but never actually drive practice
- Initiative fatigue (every year brings something new, nothing sticks)
- Inconsistent experiences for students (what's valued in one class isn't valued in another)

**In organizations, it shows up as:**

- Shifting priorities with every meeting or new leader
- Teams trying to please every stakeholder at once
- Misaligned expectations between departments
- People guessing at "what leadership wants" instead of knowing

Shared direction doesn't restrict creativity. It *frees* creativity—because it eliminates the noise. When people understand the North Star, they can innovate confidently and contribute meaningfully without constantly checking: *"Am I going the right way?"*

## The Tiny Shift

Here's the tiny shift at the heart of this chapter:

---

**FROM:** Assuming we're aligned
**TO:** Ensuring we're aligned

---

Shared direction isn't something that "just happens over time." It's something we create, test, revise, and reinforce intentionally.

The most effective teams—from kindergarten co-teachers to executive leadership groups—build shared direction around three anchors:

1. **A shared purpose** (why this matters)
2. **A shared picture of success** (what it looks like when it's working)
3. **A shared way of working** (how we'll move together)

Everything else—strategies, routines, tools—sits on top of these foundations. Without these three anchors, even good ideas drift.

## Where We Often Get Stuck

Even committed teams struggle to build shared direction. Here's why:

### 1. We Confuse Agreement with Alignment

Nodding isn't alignment.

Verbal buy-in doesn't guarantee shared meaning.

Just because people said "yes" in a meeting doesn't mean they all understood the "yes" the same way.

### 2. We Assume Others Interpret Words the Same Way We Do

"We value student agency."
"We prioritize quality service."
"We want deeper learning."

These sound great—and mean completely different things to different people. One person's "agency" is another person's "chaos." One person's "quality" is another person's "overkill."

We nod. We agree. We leave. And we all do different things.

### 3. We Move Too Quickly to Tasks

Teams often jump straight to planning—calendars, timelines, assignments—before clarifying the purpose or the criteria for success.

This creates busy work that doesn't necessarily move toward anything meaningful.

### 4. We Avoid Hard Conversations

Shared direction requires surfacing competing priorities, assumptions, and pressures.

"I need to get through the curriculum."
"I need to keep families happy."
"I need to hit our quarterly targets."

These tensions are real. But if we don't name them, they silently derail alignment. That can feel uncomfortable, so teams skip it—and the cost shows up later in confusion, resentment, or imperceptible drift.

### 5. We Think Alignment Restricts Autonomy

The fear is: *"If we narrow direction, we lose creativity."*

But it's actually the opposite.

Clear direction *expands autonomy* because people know where they have space to innovate. They're not guessing. They're creating within a frame that makes sense.

## How to Make This Shift

### 1. Start With "Why This? Why Now?"

Before planning anything—a unit, an initiative, a project, a workshop—articulate the purpose out loud.

"What is the meaningful outcome we're trying to support here?"
"What need are we responding to?"
"What does this unlock for learners, clients, or the people we serve?"

Purpose anchors people. When the "why" is clear, the "what" and "how" become easier to navigate—even when they're hard.

## 2. Define a Clear Picture of Success

A Picture of Success makes expectations visible and shared.[1]
It answers:

*"What could it look and sound like when this is working—for learners, teams, customers, or the people we serve?"*

**Strong Pictures of Success are:**

- Specific (not vague aspirations)
- Observable (you can see/hear it happening)
- Learner- or user-facing (focused on impact, not just process)
- Co-created (not handed down)

A Picture of Success doesn't micromanage. It clarifies.

It gives people a shared image of what "good" can look like—so they can make decisions aligned with that image.

**Example (classroom):**

"Students will demonstrate understanding of ecosystems by explaining interactions between organisms using evidence, visuals, and precise vocabulary."

---

1. The concept of "Pictures of Success" appears in various forms across instructional design and organizational development literature. It's similar to what some call "success criteria," "look-fors," or "shared vision."

**Example (team):**

"By the end of Q2, our onboarding process will feel seamless to clients—they'll know what to expect at each step, and 90% will report feeling confident using the platform within their first week."

The clearer the picture, the more autonomy people have to innovate within it.

## 3. Build Shared Ways of Working

These are the agreements and routines that create predictability and trust.

**Examples:**

- "We base instructional decisions on evidence of student thinking—not assumptions."
- "We test ideas in small prototypes before scaling."
- "We commit to one clear, measurable priority per quarter."
- "We check for alignment before we plan."
- "When we disagree, we name it and work through it—we don't avoid it."

These agreements make the invisible visible—and make collaboration easier.

They answer: *"How can we work together when things get hard? When we disagree? When priorities compete?"*

## 4. Pause for Meaning-Making

Don't assume everyone interprets direction the same way.

Use questions like:

"What could this look like in practice?"
"What might this mean we stop doing?"

"How could we explain this to a new colleague or team member?"
"Where could this bump up against our current habits or systems?"

This step is often skipped—and it's where alignment is actually built. Shared language emerges. Assumptions surface. Clarity deepens.

### 5. Revisit and Recalibrate Regularly

Shared direction isn't a one-and-done statement.

Teams must return to it regularly to test:

- Are we drifting?
- What's working about how we're moving together?
- What's gotten muddled?
- What needs reinforcement or revision?

A shared direction evolves—but it should never disappear.

## What This Might Look Like in Practice

### In a Primary Team

**Before designing a unit**, the team co-creates a Picture of Success:

"Students will demonstrate understanding of ecosystems by explaining interactions between organisms using evidence, visuals, and precise vocabulary."

Now the team plans assessments, learning experiences, and scaffolds aligned to this outcome—not four different versions of the unit that barely connect.

**The result:**

Students experience coherence across classrooms. Teachers feel aligned. The learning is stronger because everyone is working toward the same understanding.

## In a Secondary Science Department

**The department agrees on one shared commitment:**

"We prioritize student thinking over task completion."

They develop shared routines that reinforce this:

- Student reasoning journals
- Lab debrief protocols that focus on "why" not just "what happened"
- Think-aloud modeling
- Common question stems like "What makes you think so?" and "What's your evidence?"

**The result:**

Students experience a coherent approach to science across classes. The message is clear: *Your thinking matters here.*

## In a School Leadership Team

**The team identifies one system-wide learning priority:**

"We will strengthen the use of formative assessment to make student thinking visible."

They abandon competing initiatives. Leaders model formative assessment practices in their own meetings. Teams use the same language. Professional learning aligns around this goal.

**The result:**

Coherence grows. Teachers aren't juggling five different priorities. Energy focuses. Impact deepens.

### In a Corporate L&D Team

**The team agrees on shared direction for leadership development:**

"Our goal is to cultivate reflective, autonomy-ready leaders who can make decisions grounded in evidence and aligned with organizational values."

They create:

- A common leadership framework
- Consistent coaching questions
- Aligned onboarding modules for new leaders
- Clear measures of success

**The result:**

Every program—no matter who facilitates it—reinforces the same leadership DNA. Leaders across the organization speak a common language. The culture shifts.

## Common Pitfalls (And How to Avoid Them)

### 1. Overloading Direction With Too Many Priorities

A "shared direction" with six big goals isn't direction—it's a wishlist.

**What to try instead:** Limit yourself to 1-3 priorities. If everything is a priority, nothing actually gets the focus it needs.

### 2. Making It Too Vague to Be Useful

"We want students to be successful."

"We aim for excellence."

If you can't picture it in your mind, it's not yet shared direction.

**What to try instead:** Get specific. What might "successful" look like? What might "excellence" sound like? Make it observable.

### 3. Skipping the Sense-Making Step

Alignment doesn't come from announcement. It comes from dialogue. When people hear a direction without processing it together, they leave the room with different interpretations—and inadvertently implement different things.

**What to try instead:** Build in time for people to process, question, and clarify together. Let shared meaning emerge through conversation.

### 4. Becoming Rigid

Shared direction should guide, not box people in. When a direction is treated as fixed rather than *living,* people stop adapting to new information. Compliance replaces genuine commitment.

**What to try instead:** Revisit regularly. Adapt when needed. Hold the "why" tightly; hold the "how" more loosely.

### 5. Letting Old Habits Override New Commitments

Without regular check-ins, drift is inevitable.

**What to try instead:** Build in reflection points. "Are we still aligned with what we said mattered? What's getting in the way?"

## Tiny Shift: Try This Tomorrow

Before your next team meeting or planning session, ask everyone to write a one-sentence answer to: **"What might success look like for this work right now?"**

Share the answers. Compare them. Notice:

- Where definitions align
- Where assumptions differ
- Where clarity is missing

Take five minutes to co-create one shared statement.

It's astonishing how quickly a team shifts from scattered to aligned when they see the same horizon.

## Reflection Prompts

1. When has a lack of shared direction slowed down or confused your work? What did that cost you?

2. What assumptions are currently shaping your team's understanding of "success"? Are they shared—or silently diverging?

3. Where might people be interpreting the same words in completely different ways?

4. What shared agreements could make collaboration smoother and reduce friction?

5. What's one place where establishing clearer shared direction could unlock stronger agency for learners, team members, or the people you serve?

6. How often do you return to your stated priorities to check: *Are we still aligned? Or have we drifted?*

## Closing Note

Shared direction isn't about control. It's about coherence.

It creates a collective sense of purpose and a shared definition of success. It lets people contribute with confidence. It amplifies impact while reducing unnecessary friction.

Perhaps most importantly, shared direction tells people:

> *"We're moving together. We know where we're going. And your thinking matters in getting us there."*

**Agency grows inside clarity.** That clarity doesn't restrict freedom—it creates the container where freedom becomes purposeful.

---

With this chapter, Part I comes full circle.

We've explored how agency thrives not in isolation, but in interdependence. How it grows when we value thinking over compliance. How it strengthens when we measure what actually matters. How it deepens when learning is active, not passive. And now, how it gains momentum when everyone is moving in the same direction—not because they're controlled, but because they're aligned.

**Agency doesn't flourish in isolation. It flourishes in clarity, purpose, and shared commitment.**

That's the foundation.

Now let's look at the daily moves that bring it to life.

# PART TWO
# THE DAILY MOVES
## TINY SHIFTS THAT BUILD AGENCY IN LEARNING, WORK, AND LEADERSHIP

The belief shifts in Part I matter—they change how we see people, learning, and work. But beliefs alone don't change much. We need daily practices that make those beliefs *real.*

This section is about the moves you can make tomorrow. Small, specific, sustainable changes that build agency into the rhythm of how you teach, lead, facilitate, and collaborate. And here's something worth saying clearly: You don't have to have the beliefs fully sorted before you begin. Sometimes the move comes first—and the belief catches up through the doing.

These six chapters cover a range of territory: how we design learning and work, how we build safe conditions for voice and choice, how we ask questions, how we make thinking visible, how we pace ourselves, and how we see the people we work with. You don't need to implement all of them at once. Start where your context needs you most.

These aren't one-time interventions. They're habits. Routines. Ways of working that, over time, transform culture—not because you were handed a mandate from above, but because you made a series of small, deliberate decisions about how to show up.

Let's begin.

# CHAPTER 6

## DESIGN WITH PEOPLE, NOT FOR THEM

### Opening Scene

Picture this: It's Monday morning in a Grade 5 classroom. The teacher unveils a beautifully laminated poster titled "Our New Inquiry Project: Ancient Civilizations."

She spent all weekend perfecting it. The essential question is clear. The timeline is detailed. The assessment rubric is thorough. Even the group assignments are done.

Students lean forward ... for about six seconds.

Then the questions start:

"Wait—why are we doing ancient civilizations?"
"Do we get to choose our groups?"
"Can we study a different civilization than the ones on the list?"
"Do we have to follow all these steps?"

The teacher sighs. She thought clarity would create excitement. Instead, she's spending more energy convincing than teaching.

Now shift the scene.

A project manager at a healthcare nonprofit rolls out a new workflow to her team. The presentation is polished. The timeline is tight. The expectations are crystal-clear. She's thought of everything.

People nod politely.

But afterward, someone whispers in the hallway: "This will never work with our actual caseload."

Another colleague adds: "Why didn't they ask us before building all this?"

The plan slowly dissolves in a mix of quiet frustration and work-around culture.

---

Different spaces. Same dynamic.

Well-intentioned design. Low collective ownership. And that's the paradox: The more fully formed our plans are when we bring them to others, the harder it is for those people to feel any real ownership of them.

Agency doesn't flourish when we present people with beautifully polished plans. Agency flourishes when they can actually shape the plan with us.

## Why This Matters

Most teachers, leaders, and managers genuinely want people to feel empowered. But empowerment—real empowerment—requires something many systems are not built for:

**Letting people influence the thing they're part of.**

Too often, we unintentionally design learning and work *for* people instead of *with* them. And the consequences are predictable:

- Students comply but don't invest.
- Teachers implement but don't commit.

- Teams execute but don't innovate.

When people don't get to shape the work, they rarely feel connected to it.

The truth is this: **Ownership can't be handed to someone. It has to be built *with* them.**

When we shift from designing *for* people to designing *with* them, a few things happen:

- Engagement becomes real, not performative
- Solutions fit the context, not just the theory
- People feel capable, not controlled
- Creativity increases—because people have permission to bring their ideas forward
- Accountability strengthens—because people are committed to what they helped shape

Designing with people isn't slower. It's smarter. And ultimately, it's the only way to build agency that lasts.

## The Tiny Shift

Here's the tiny shift at the heart of this chapter:

---

**FROM:** "I designed this for you"
**TO:** "We designed this together"

---

**Design *for* says:** "I already figured out what's best. I need you to follow it."

**Design *with* says:** "We'll shape this so it works for the people who will actually live it."

Design *for* feels efficient upfront but creates resistance later.

Design *with* takes a little longer upfront but creates engagement, clarity, and momentum that last.

When you design with people:

- They see their fingerprints in the work
- They understand the purpose behind decisions
- They feel respected and trusted
- They build skills in problem-solving, planning, and reflection
- They bring their strengths to the table—strengths you would never have accessed on your own

**Agency isn't the outcome of perfect design. It's the outcome of shared design.**

## How to Make This Shift

### 1. Start by Sharing the Constraints, Not the Plan

Most of us begin with a near-finished plan and then ask people what they think. By then, the window for genuine influence is already closed.

A better starting point: "Here are the boundaries we have to work within. Within those, let's design this together."

**In classrooms:**

"We need to demonstrate our understanding of ecosystems. Within that, what kinds of projects would you like to create?"

**In teams:**

"The deadline is fixed and the deliverable is non-negotiable. But the workflow, roles, and process? We can shape those together."

**In professional learning:**

"Here's what we need to accomplish by the end of this session.

How we get there—and what examples we use—we can decide together."

Constraints actually increase creativity—when people know where they can play.

## 2. Co-Create the Questions Before Co-Creating the Plan

Most people skip straight to designing the "what" and "how." But shared design starts with *shared inquiry.*

Try beginning with questions like:

- "What do we want this experience to achieve—for learners, for families, for our team?"
- "What would make this meaningful?"
- "What do we already know will be tricky, and how might we work around that?"
- "What would success feel like for us?"

You're not co-designing the details yet. You're co-designing the direction. Once people have shaped the questions, shaping the answers comes naturally.

## 3. Use Quick, Lightweight Structures

You don't need a multi-week participatory design process (though that can be powerful, too). Small structures are enough:

- Idea dump → pattern spotting → deciding next steps
- Sketching possible workflows on sticky notes
- Silent idea generation followed by group synthesis
- 1-2-4-All (think alone → pairs → groups of four → whole group)
- Dot voting on options
- Plus/Delta (What's working? What needs to change?)

Design *with* doesn't mean hours lost in endless conversation. It means making thinking visible so the group can shape it together.

### 4. Build in "Invisible Choices"

Even when the big decisions are fixed, there are always choices people can influence. Invisible choices might include:

- Which examples to use
- How to prototype the first step
- How to group or sequence work
- What tools or texts to select
- How to share learning or progress
- What supports or check-ins people want
- How communication should flow
- What success criteria should emphasize

Naming those choices out loud matters. Otherwise, people assume everything is pre-decided.

"I'm holding these three things. Everything else? We can shape together."

### 5. Close the Loop with Transparency

Design *with* only works when people see how their input shaped the outcome.

You might say:

"Here's what I heard from you ...
Here's what we can act on now ...
Here's what we'll revisit later ...
Here's what we can't change—and why."

That final piece—explaining *why*—is the trust-builder. People don't need total control. They need honest clarity.

## What This Might Look Like in Practice

### In a Grade 3 Classroom

**The situation:**

A teacher wants to improve her math centers. In the past, she designed new rotations alone based on what she thought students needed.

**The shift:**

Instead, she brings students into the process:

"What helps you learn best in centers?"
"What makes some centers harder to stay focused in?"
"What routines feel smooth? What routines feel bumpy?"

Students brainstorm. They sort ideas. They identify patterns.

Together, they redesign three routines and co-create a simple success rubric.

**The result:**

The teacher still curates the math tasks—that's her expertise. But the students shaped the conditions for how learning will work. Ownership grows not from choosing activities, but from designing how learning happens.

### In a Secondary Math Department

**The situation:**

The department was seeing inconsistent results across classes. The head's usual response was a standardized fix: same pacing guide, same problem sets, same formative checks. Teachers complied. The gaps persisted.

**The shift:**

This time, before designing any solution, she brings the team together around the data: "What patterns are you seeing in your own classrooms? Where do students tend to get stuck, and where are they surprising you?"

Teachers who'd been quietly solving problems alone started naming them out loud. Rather than standardizing a fix, the head facilitates two shared commitments the team will hold in common—and creates space for teachers to adapt everything else based on what they're learning.

**The result:**

The approach that emerges is stronger than anything she would have designed alone. Teachers take it seriously—not because they were told to, but because their thinking shaped it.

### In a Nonprofit Program Team

**The situation:**

A program director noticed attendance at her after-school sessions slipping. Her instinct was to redesign the curriculum herself—sharpen the objectives, add a stronger hook.

**The shift:**

Instead, she asked staff to run three short listening conversations with participants:

- What here actually matters to you?
- What feels like a waste of time?

- What do you wish existed?

She held the constraints clearly—budget and schedule weren't moving—but told her team: "The content and format aren't mine to decide alone. You're closer to this than I am."

What emerged included a peer-led component, a simple choice structure, and a session format staff flagged as far more sustainable to deliver well.

**The result:**

Participation steadied. One staff member reflected: "I'd been noticing some of this for months. I didn't think it was my place to say so."

The director didn't step back; she held the frame and made the final call. But the design belonged to more than one person—and it showed.

### In a Corporate Training Environment

**The situation:**

A leadership workshop used to be delivered as a fully scripted experience. Facilitators covered the content. Participants took notes. Application was inconsistent.

**The shift:**

The facilitator builds co-design moments into the workshop:

- Participants identify their real team dilemmas (not hypotheticals)
- They co-create success criteria for effective leadership conversations
- They choose which case studies to analyze based on relevance to their work
- They co-own how they'll apply learning back on the job

**The result:**

The facilitator provides structure and expertise. Participants shape the experience so it serves their actual context.

One leader shared: "I thought this would tell me the right answers. Instead, it helped me think better about my actual challenges."

### In a Coaching Conversation

**The situation:**

A coach meets with a school leader who's struggling with meeting culture. In the past, the coach would offer best practices and strategies.

**The shift:**

Instead, the coach asks:
"What do you want people to experience in your meetings?"
"What gets in the way of that?"
"What do your staff already do well that we can build on?"
Together, they draft a few small experiments to try.

**The result:**

The leader feels like a partner in problem-solving—not a recipient of advice. The solutions are more likely to stick because they were co-created, not prescribed.

## Common Pitfalls (And How to Avoid Them)

### 1. Pretend Choice

Inviting people to "shape" something that's already fully decided erodes trust faster than not asking at all.

**What to try instead:** Only invite input where there's genuine room for influence. Be transparent about what's fixed and what's flexible.

### 2. Too Many Options

Democratizing every decision creates fatigue. Not everything needs to be co-designed.

**What to try instead:** Be strategic. Co-design the things that most affect people's daily work or learning. Hold some decisions yourself.

### 3. Letting Perfect Get in the Way of Progress

Co-design isn't a quest for ideal consensus. It's about creating meaningful influence.

**What to try instead:** Aim for "good enough together" rather than "perfect alone."

### 4. Assuming Silence Means Agreement

People may hold back if they feel the decision is already made—even if you say it's not.

**What to try instead:** Use structures that draw thinking out. Written reflections before discussion. Small groups before whole group. Anonymous input if needed.

### 5. Overcorrecting Into Chaos

Design *with* doesn't mean everyone decides everything. It means people influence the parts they actually live.

**What to try instead:** Be clear about who holds which decisions, where input is welcomed, and how the final call will be made.

## Tiny Shift: Try This Tomorrow

Pick an upcoming lesson, meeting, or workflow. Before you finalize your plan, ask the group:

**"What would make this most useful for you?"**

or

**"What's one thing we should consider before we finalize this?"**

Invite ideas. Capture them visibly (whiteboard, chart paper, shared doc).

Integrate at least one suggestion into the design. Then name it when you do: "We added this because you said it would help."

That's how shared design becomes real.

## Reflection Prompts

1. Where in your current work do you tend to design alone? What drives that choice?

2. Who is most impacted by your next plan or initiative? How might they shape it with you?

3. What constraints are truly fixed in your context—and what's flexible inside them?

4. When have you personally felt the most ownership over a project or learning experience? What created that feeling?

5. Which part of your design process could you open up this week—just a little—to invite others in?

6. What might it take to build a culture where co-design is expected, not exceptional?

## Closing Note

Designing with people isn't about giving up expertise. It's about using your expertise to create the conditions for other people's expertise to matter.

When we invite students, colleagues, and teams into the design process:

- We get better ideas
- We create more sustainable systems
- We build trust and capability
- We grow leaders at every level

Most of all, we send a powerful message:

**"You belong here. Your thinking matters. We're building this together."**

That's where agency stops being a buzzword and becomes the heartbeat of how we learn and work.

# CHAPTER 7

## BUILD ROUTINES THAT MAKE CHOICE SAFE

### Opening Scene

It's the start of the day in a Grade 1 classroom in Beijing. Kids file in from the hallway, hang backpacks on hooks, and gather on the rug without anyone reminding them. They know the rhythm.

**Greeting.**

**Share.**

**Activity.**

**Message.**

They've done this hundreds of times. And today, when the teacher asks, "Who'd like to try leading the greeting?" five hands shoot up—including hands from kids who usually whisper, not volunteer.

Why? Not because they suddenly became brave. Because the structure made contribution feel normal.

---

Now shift the scene.

A product team logs into their daily stand-up on Zoom. Different time zones, different locations, same familiar pattern:

**What I did yesterday.**

**What I'm doing today.**

**What's blocking me.**

They've done it hundreds of times. But lately something new keeps happening.

A quiet engineer says, "I'm stuck on the integration and I need help."

A junior designer adds, "I made a mistake on the prototype yesterday—can someone review it with me?"

No drama. No judgment. Just routine transparency.

---

Both spaces have something crucial in common:

> **People are taking small risks because the structure makes it feel normal—not brave.**

Choice isn't inherently safe. Voice isn't naturally easy. Risk-taking doesn't magically appear when you hang a poster about agency on the wall.

People step forward when the rhythms around them say: *"This is a place where trying, questioning, and not knowing are expected."*

Predictability fuels courage. When people know what will happen next—how they'll be invited to participate, what's expected, who goes when—the nervous system stops scanning for threat and starts making room for thinking.

**Psychological safety isn't the absence of fear. It's the presence of routines that make courage feel doable.**

Amy Edmondson's groundbreaking research on psychological safety shows that people take more risks, share more ideas, and perform better when they trust they won't be punished for mistakes or questions.[1] But that safety doesn't come from declarations—it comes

1. Edmondson, A. (1999). "Psychological Safety and Learning Behavior in Work Teams," *Administrative Science Quarterly*, 44(2), 350-383.

from consistent patterns and structures.

## Why This Matters

When schools or organizations say they want more agency, they often start with the exciting parts: choice boards, flexible seating, self-directed projects, innovation time, hackathons.

Those tools can be wonderful—but only when the soil is right.

In many environments, the unspoken story is:

"You can make choices ... as long as they're right."
"You can take risks ... as long as they work."
"You can share ideas ... as long as they match mine."

People pick up on that quickly. Students stay quiet. Teachers stick to the script. Teams avoid naming problems until they've grown too big. Employees wait for permission.

We misdiagnose the issue as a lack of confidence, initiative, or creativity. But underneath is something simpler and far more human:

**People don't avoid choice because they're incapable. They avoid choice because it feels unsafe.**

And psychological safety isn't built through pep talks or posters. *It's built through routines*—tiny, predictable structures that make risk-taking feel normal and shared.

When routines are predictable, shared, and purposeful, they become what researchers call "liberating structures"—containers that support people just enough to give them the courage to take risks.[2]

That's the paradox at the heart of agency: **Learners don't need**

2. Henri Lipmanowicz and Keith McCandless developed Liberating Structures as practical facilitation methods building on William Torbert's theory of organizational structures that support shared purpose and self-direction (Torbert, W.R., 1978, "Educating Toward Shared Purpose, Self-Direction, and Quality Work: The Theory and Practice of Liberating Structure," *Journal of Higher Education*, 49(6), 560-585; Lipmanowicz & McCandless, 2013).

**endless freedom; they need steady rhythms that make participation feel safe.**

When the structure liberates rather than restricts, voice rises and agency expands. Meaningful routines don't just encourage voice. They expect it. They hold it up. They protect it.

**Agency grows when:**

- The environment is predictable enough for people to step forward
- The expectations are clear enough to lower the emotional cost of trying
- The structures are sturdy enough to catch people when they wobble

This is the quiet architecture of agency. And it begins with routines.

## The Tiny Shift

Here's the tiny shift at the heart of this chapter:

---

**FROM:** Offering choice occasionally
**TO:** Building routines that make choice safe every day

---

Choice by itself is fragile. Choice inside a reliable structure becomes powerful.

**Without safety:**

- Choice feels like exposure
- Voice feels like risk
- Mistakes feel like threats

**With safety:**

- Choice feels like participation
- Voice feels like contribution
- Mistakes feel like information

Psychological safety isn't a vibe. It's a pattern.

When people know what will happen, who goes when, how they'll be treated, and what support looks like, their nervous systems calm down enough to try things.

**Routines are the scaffolds that make agency possible.**

## How to Make This Shift

### 1. Make Participation Predictable

Uncertainty is the enemy of voice. Predictable rhythms lower the stakes.

Try routines like:

**In classrooms:**

- "Turn and learn" conversations every 5-7 minutes during lessons
- "Symphony share" where everyone speaks once (in any order, but everyone contributes)
- A predictable question pattern: "What do you notice? What do you think? What do you wonder?"
- Daily or weekly reflection prompts at consistent times

**In meetings:**

- Check-ins at the start: "One word about how you're arriving today"
- Round-robin sharing where everyone gets 60 seconds

- Consistent closing: "What's one takeaway you're leaving with?"

**In teams:**

- Weekly retros with the same format (What went well? What didn't? What will we try?)
- Predictable 1-on-1 rhythms with consistent questions

Predictability helps quieter voices because they don't have to wonder: *"Will I be called on randomly? Will I be put on the spot? Will I have to fight for space?"*

**Tiny start:** Announce the participation pattern before you begin.

"First we'll think alone for 60 seconds, then we'll talk in pairs, then we'll share as a group."

Confidence rises when uncertainty drops.

## 2. Build Routines That Normalize Not Knowing

If people feel pressured to be right, they stop taking risks.

Create rituals where uncertainty is welcomed:

**In classrooms:**

- "My question today is … "
- "The part I'm wrestling with is … "
- "Here's where my understanding fell apart … "
- "I tried this strategy and it didn't work—here's what I learned … "

**In teams:**

- Weekly "blocker roundtables" where naming what's stuck is the point

- "Learning moments" where people share productive failures
- "Assumptions we're testing" visible on a shared board

**In professional learning:**

- "One thing that surprised me ... "
- "Something I'm still figuring out ... "

When you normalize not knowing, you unlock the door to agency.

## 3. Use Structures That Spread Voice, Not Spotlight It

Big open questions like "Any thoughts?" usually privilege the boldest voices. Use routines that democratize contribution:

- **Sentence starters** that help people begin
- **Silent brainstorming** followed by group synthesis
- **Anonymous idea collection** (digital tools, index cards)
- **Timed rounds** where everyone gets equal time
- **Role-based rotations** (facilitator, summarizer, skeptic, supporter, questioner)

These routines communicate: *"Everyone belongs here. Everyone contributes. No one dominates."*

Agency is collective, not competitive.

## 4. Anchor Routines in Shared Agreements

Routines work best when people co-create the norms around them. Have groups name:

- "What does respectful disagreement look like here?"
- "What do we do when someone gets stuck?"
- "How do we repair when we misstep?"
- "How do we support risk-taking?"

Post these agreements. Return to them. Revise them when needed.

Routines without agreements can feel mechanical. Routines with agreements are empowering.

### 5. Close the Loop Every Time

Psychological safety grows when people see their voices have an impact. After any routine involving contribution, do a quick closing loop:

- "What we heard ... "
- "What we'll take forward ... "
- "What we'll revise based on your input ... "
- "What questions we'll return to next time ... "

When people see their voices shaping the work, they trust the routine more deeply.

This step is easy to skip when time is short. Don't. People can tolerate having their ideas adapted or set aside—but they rarely recover from never finding out what happened to them at all. The loop closes that gap. It transforms *"I contributed"* into *"I mattered here."* And that is the difference between a routine people endure and one they genuinely trust.

## What This Might Look Like in Practice

### In a Grade 3 Classroom

**The situation:**

During Writers' Workshop, students struggled with peer feedback. Comments were either unhelpfully vague ("Good job!") or accidentally hurtful ("This doesn't make sense").

**The shift:**

The teacher introduced **co-constructed success criteria**—a research-informed practice where students help define what quality looks like before they create.[3]

Before starting a new writing piece, she asked: "What makes a strong lead? Let's look at three examples and figure it out together."

Students analyzed mentor texts, identified patterns, and built criteria in their own words:

- Hooks the reader with a question, action, or surprising detail
- Gives just enough information (not too much, not too little)
- Makes you want to keep reading

**The result:**

When students gave each other feedback, they referenced the shared criteria they'd built together. Comments became specific: "Your lead has a great question, but I'm not sure what the story's about yet."

Because students understood what quality looked like—and had shaped that understanding themselves—feedback became genuinely helpful instead of performative. The routine didn't just change behavior—it changed culture.

## In a Secondary Science Class

**The situation:**

Students rarely asked questions unless they were absolutely sure they were "smart" questions.

---

3. Co-constructing success criteria is a core formative assessment practice supported by extensive research (Hattie & Clarke, 2018; Wiliam, 2018). When students help define quality standards before creating work, they develop clearer understanding of learning goals and stronger capacity for self-assessment.

**The shift:**

The teacher introduced a weekly ritual: *"My Best Wrong Idea of the Week."* One student shares a misconception they had—and how their thinking shifted.

Soon, students compete to bring in the "best wrong idea." The classroom erupts in conversation about how learning actually happens.

**The result:**

Curiosity rises. Risk-taking normalizes. Agency builds—because being wrong became part of learning, not a sign of failure.

## In a School Leadership Team

**The situation:**

Team meetings drifted into long monologues from whoever spoke first. Quieter voices rarely contributed. Decisions felt top-heavy.

**The shift:**

The leader implemented a structure:

Three minutes silent writing → Three minutes sharing in pairs → Group synthesis

**The result:**
Within a month:

- More people contributed
- Decisions were smarter (they included more perspectives)
- Teachers felt heard
- The principal wasn't carrying the whole cognitive load alone

Routines redistributed leadership.

### In a Corporate Team

**The situation:**

A product team struggled with hidden blockers. Deadlines slipped, but nobody admitted where they were stuck. Asking for help felt like admitting failure.

**The shift:**

A manager introduced a new norm in stand-ups:

After each person's update, the rest of the team asks: "What support do you need?"

**The result:**

Blockers moved from secret problems to shared puzzles. The team became more interdependent. Performance improved—because psychological safety improved.

## Common Pitfalls (And How to Avoid Them)

### 1. Confusing Freedom with Safety

More choice does not automatically equal more agency. Without safety, more choice just equals more stress.

**What to try instead:** Build routines first. Then expand choice within those routines.

### 2. Overengineering the Routines

When routines get too complicated, they stop being supportive and start being exhausting. A routine that requires a flowchart to explain won't survive contact with a real Monday morning.

**What to try instead:** Keep it simple. Three steps, not ten. Clear language, not jargon.

### 3. Assuming Safety Once It's Named

Psychological safety is *experienced,* not declared. You can post norms on the wall and open every meeting with an invitation to share—but what people actually watch is what happens to the first person who takes a risk.

**What to try instead:** Build safety through *living* repetition and reinforcement, not speeches.

### 4. Ignoring Power Dynamics

If leaders or teachers dominate the "safe spaces," people stop believing the routine.

**What to try instead:** Model vulnerability. Share your own struggles. Speak last, not first.

### 5. Dropping Routines When Things Get Busy

Ironically, people need routines most when pressure is high.

**What to try instead:** Protect routines like you'd protect oxygen. Consistency is its own form of safety.

## Tiny Shift: Try This Tomorrow

Pick one upcoming lesson or meeting. Add one predictable participation routine:

- **"Think → Pair → Share"** with a visible 30-second timer
- **"One insight, one question"** at the end
- A quick **"How are you arriving today?"** temperature check
- A structured round: **"What do you need to keep moving forward?"**

Don't overhaul everything. Just create one rhythm that tells people: *"You belong. Your voice matters. You won't be punished for trying."*

That's how agency begins to feel safe enough to practice.

## Reflection Prompts

1. Where do people in your space seem hesitant to speak, choose, or try? What might that hesitation be protecting?

2. Which routines in your day already support safety—and which might unintentionally undermine it?

3. How predictable is participation in your classroom, team, or organization? Who consistently gets space to contribute, and who doesn't?

4. What routines could help normalize uncertainty and struggle instead of hiding them?

5. If you built one new routine that protected voice and risk-taking, what might you start noticing within a week?

6. When was the last time you modeled not knowing something? How did it shift the energy in the room?

## Closing Note

Agency is often imagined as bold, dramatic action. But in reality, agency builds steadily—through small, sturdy routines that make risk feel survivable.

When people know:

- What to expect
- How to participate
- That their voice will be welcomed
- That mistakes won't cost them belonging

They step forward more often. They contribute more fully. They take the kind of risks that lead to growth.

**Routines don't restrict agency. They create the container where agency can breathe.** Because when safety becomes the norm, courage becomes contagious. And that's when people—students, teachers, teams, leaders—start showing you who they've been capable of being all along.

# CHAPTER 8

## ASK BETTER QUESTIONS (AND FEWER OF THEM)

### Opening Scene

It's a classroom discussion. Technically "interactive." The teacher calls on student after student. Hands shoot up. Questions fly:

"What's the main idea?"
"What's the definition of this word?"
"What page is that on?"
"Who remembers what we did yesterday?"

The same three students answer every time. Others stop listening—there's no need. Someone else will get called on.

Questions come quickly. Answers come quickly.

But thinking? It barely shows up.

---

Now shift the scene.

It's a leadership meeting. The facilitator is trying to be inclusive, asking lots of questions:

"Any questions?"
"Does that make sense?"
"Are we all aligned?"
"Everyone good?"

Heads nod. No one speaks.

The facilitator moves on, reassured. But afterward, in the hallway, the real questions surface:

"Wait—what are we actually deciding?"
"Do we have any say in this?"
"I wasn't sure if that was rhetorical or not."

---

Different settings. Same problem.

Lots of questions. Very little thinking.

We tend to believe that more questions automatically mean more engagement. But the truth is quieter—and more uncomfortable: **Not all questions invite agency. Some questions shut it down.**

## Why This Matters

Questions shape who holds the thinking.

In many learning spaces—classrooms, meetings, workshops, boardrooms—the person asking the questions is doing most of the cognitive work.

Deciding what matters.

Deciding when to move on.

Deciding which answers count.

Deciding who speaks—and for how long.

Even when participation looks high, ownership can be low. Why? Because rapid-fire questioning often trains people to:

- Wait for prompts
- Guess what the asker wants

- Offer short, safe responses
- Hand the thinking back as quickly as possible

Over time, people learn: *My job is to respond. Your job is to think.* And that's the opposite of agency.

Agency grows when people are trusted to:

- Sit with uncertainty
- Frame problems themselves
- Generate questions—not just answers
- Decide what deserves attention

But that requires restraint. It requires fewer questions—and better ones.

## The Tiny Shift

Here's the tiny shift at the heart of this chapter:

---

**FROM:** Asking many questions
**TO:** Asking questions that liberate thinking

---

Not questions that check for recall.

Not questions that funnel people toward a predetermined answer.

Not questions that simply keep the pace moving.

But instead: **questions that slow the moment, hand the thinking over, and create space for meaning-making, disagreement, and choice.**

When we ask fewer, better questions:

- We stop performing curiosity and start practicing it
- We reduce cognitive noise and increase cognitive depth
- We make room for learners, teams, and communities to think beyond us

**Agency doesn't come from being questioned constantly. It comes from being *trusted* with the question itself.**

## How to Make This Shift

### 1. Notice Who the Questions Are For

Many questions are actually for the questioner—not the learner.

They help us check understanding. They help us keep control. They help us feel like something is happening.

Try pausing and asking yourself: *"Who does this question serve?"*

If the answer is:

**Me** → consider whether it needs to be asked aloud.
**Them** → consider whether it needs more space.

Sometimes the most powerful move is to ask one question—and then get out of the way.

### 2. Trade Recall Questions for Meaning Questions

Recall questions keep thinking shallow. Meaning questions open it up.

**Instead of:** "What's the right answer?"

**Try:**

- "What do you notice?"
- "What feels unclear or unresolved here?"
- "What's one interpretation you're wrestling with?"
- "What feels important—and why?"
- "Where does your thinking bump up against someone else's?"

These questions don't rush closure. They invite thinking to surface in different forms—and that signals trust.

### 3. Build in Real Wait Time (Longer Than Feels Comfortable)

Agency doesn't live in speed. When questions come too fast, only the quickest processors respond. Everyone else opts out.

**Try this:**

Ask one question.
Pause.
Count silently to ten.
Let the discomfort do its work.

**You'll notice:**

- More voices enter
- Responses deepen
- People stop performing and start thinking

Silence isn't a failure. It's often where agency begins.

### 4. Ask Questions That Don't Belong to You

Some questions should not be answered by the person in charge.

**Try offering questions back to the group:**

- "What should we be paying attention to here?"
- "What feels most worth discussing?"
- "What's the real problem we're trying to solve?"
- "What questions are you carrying right now?"

When people help frame the inquiry, they invest differently. They lean in. They take responsibility. They stay.

### 5. Let Questions Replace Instructions (Sometimes)

Instructions tell people what to do. Questions invite them to decide how to proceed.

**Instead of:** "Follow these steps … "

**Try:**

- "How might you approach this?"
- "What options do you see?"
- "What would make this work better?"
- "If you got stuck, where would you look for help?"

This doesn't mean removing all structure. It means using structure as a container—not a script.

## What This Might Look Like in Practice

### In an Upper Elementary Classroom

**The situation:**

A teacher noticed she was asking over fifty questions in a single lesson—most of them yes/no or recall-based. Students were answering, but not thinking deeply.

**The shift:**

She made one change: She planned three questions for the entire lesson. Each was open. Each required explanation. Each invited multiple perspectives.

**The result:**

Students talked longer. They built on one another's ideas. They disagreed—productively. The teacher spoke less—and learned more about what her students actually understood.

## In a Middle School Humanities Class

**The situation:**

After reading a text, the teacher used to ask comprehension questions to check understanding. Students gave surface-level answers.

**The shift:**

Instead, she asked: "What feels unsettled here? What's the question this text is raising for you?"

Students generated their own questions. The class discussion followed their curiosity—not a worksheet.

**The result:**

Engagement deepened. Ownership grew. Students weren't hunting for the teacher's interpretation—they were constructing their own.

## In a Leadership Team Meeting

**The situation:**

A principal used to end meetings with: "Any questions?"

Silence. Every time.

**The shift:**

She replaced it with: "What concerns should we surface before moving forward?"

**The result:**

The tone shifted immediately. Real questions emerged. Hard conversations happened earlier—when they could still shape decisions instead of derailing them later.

### In a Professional Learning Session

**The situation:**

A facilitator used to deliver content-heavy slide decks. Participants were polite but disengaged.

**The shift:**

She replaced most of the content with one opening question: "What's one tension you're experiencing in your practice right now?"

The room leaned in. The learning became immediately relevant. The expertise in the room showed up.

**The result:**

Participants weren't just receiving information—they were applying it to real challenges. Transfer increased. Impact deepened.

## Common Pitfalls (And How to Avoid Them)

### 1. Asking Leading Questions

If the answer is already decided, agency is an illusion.

**What to try instead:** Ask questions you're genuinely curious about. If you already know the answer you want, you're testing—not inquiring.

### 2. Filling Every Silence

Thinking needs oxygen.

**What to try instead:** Count to ten. Let silence do its work. Resist the urge to rescue people from productive struggle.

### 3. Confusing Curiosity with Control

More questions don't equal more openness—especially if you're still controlling where the thinking goes.

**What to try instead:** Release control of the direction. Let the thinking emerge from the group.

### 4. Asking for Questions but Punishing Honesty

People notice what happens to the first brave voice. If someone asks a hard question and gets dismissed, redirected, or subtly penalized, others draw the conclusion instantly. The invitation was theater. The space wasn't actually safe.

**What to try instead:** Welcome hard questions. Thank people for naming what's difficult or unclear.

### 5. Treating Questioning as a Technique Instead of a Stance

This is about trust, not tricks.

**What to try instead:** Cultivate genuine curiosity. Questions flow naturally when you're truly interested in what people think.

## Tiny Shift: Try This Tomorrow

Look at your next lesson, meeting, or session.

**Reduce your questions by half.**

Then choose one question that:

- Has more than one possible answer
- Can't be rushed
- Genuinely shapes what happens next

Ask it. Pause. Listen.
Let the thinking belong to the people in the room.

## Reflection Prompts

1. Where do you tend to over-question in order to maintain control?
2. Which of your questions are about checking—and which are about meaning-making?
3. Who speaks most often after you ask a question? Who rarely speaks—and why might that be?
4. How do you respond when answers don't go where you expected? What might your response teach people about what's valued?
5. What's one question you could stop asking—and one better question you could start asking instead?
6. What could change if you asked half as many questions—but made each one count?

## Closing Note

Questions are powerful. But only when they make space—not noise. Agency doesn't grow from being constantly prompted. It grows when people are trusted to think, wonder, and decide.

Ask fewer questions. Ask braver ones. And then: step back.

**That's where the thinking lives—and that's where agency begins.**

# CHAPTER 9

## MAKE THINKING VISIBLE

### Opening Scene

It's independent work time in a classroom. Students are busy. Pencils moving. Screens glowing. Pages filling up.

From the outside, it looks productive.

The teacher circulates:

"Nice work."
"Keep going."
"Looks good."

But later, when she collects the work, something troubling becomes clear: Several students arrived at the same answer using completely different reasoning—some sound, some flawed. A few followed a strategy without understanding it. Others had rich ideas but no clear way to show them.

*The work hid the thinking.*

---

Now shift the scene.

A strategy meeting wraps up. The team agrees on a plan. Decisions are documented. Action items are assigned. Everyone leaves feeling aligned.

Weeks later, implementation stalls. Confusion creeps in. Tension rises.

Someone finally asks: "Wait—why did we decide this in the first place?"

No one is quite sure.

*The reasoning never made it into the room*—at least not in a way others could see or revisit.

---

Different spaces. Same issue.

When thinking stays invisible, learning becomes fragile. Decisions become shallow. Agency begins to recede.

## Why This Matters

Agency depends on thinking being seen, named, and valued.

Ron Ritchhart and his colleagues at Project Zero have spent decades researching what they call "making thinking visible"—the practice of externalizing cognitive processes so they can be examined, shared, and refined.[1] Their work shows that when thinking becomes visible, learning deepens, misconceptions surface earlier, and students develop metacognitive awareness.

But many systems only reward outputs:

- The right answer
- The finished product
- The polished plan
- The completed task

---

1. Ritchhart, R., Church, M., & Morrison, K. (2011). *Making Thinking Visible: How to Promote Engagement, Understanding, and Independence for All Learners*. Jossey-Bass.

We rarely ask:

- How did you arrive there?
- What did you consider?
- What did you rule out?
- What changed your mind?

**When thinking remains hidden:**

- Misconceptions go unnoticed
- Surface-level understanding gets mistaken for mastery
- People learn to perform, not reason
- Decision-making becomes opaque—and unchallengeable

And over time, people internalize a message: *My thinking doesn't matter—only the result does.* That message is corrosive to agency.

Agency grows when people see their thinking taken seriously—even when it's unfinished, messy, or imperfect.

## The Tiny Shift

Here's the tiny shift at the heart of this chapter:

---

**FROM:** Valuing answers (invisible cognition)

**TO:** Valuing the *thinking* behind the answers (shared, examinable thinking)

---

When we make thinking visible:[2]

- We normalize learning as a process, not a performance

2. This draws heavily on the work of Ron Ritchhart and Project Zero at Harvard. See Ritchhart, R., Church, M., & Morrison, K. (2011). *Making Thinking Visible: How to Promote Engagement, Understanding, and Independence for All Learners*. Jossey-Bass.

- We surface misunderstandings early—before they harden
- We make it safer to revise ideas
- We create shared language for growth
- We help people see patterns in how they think

Visibility isn't about surveillance. It's about *understanding*—and understanding is the foundation of agency.

## How to Make This Shift

### 1. Ask for Reasoning Before Results

The order matters. When we ask for answers first, thinking collapses into correctness. When we ask for reasoning first, understanding expands.

**Try prompts like:**

- "Walk me through how you're thinking about this."
- "What led you here?"
- "What did you try before this?"
- "What assumptions are you making?"

**In meetings:**

- "What data or experience is shaping your view?"
- "What trade-offs did you consider?"
- "What would need to be true for this to work?"

When reasoning leads, answers become learning opportunities—not verdicts.

### 2. Create Artifacts That Capture Thinking

Thinking needs a place to live. That might look like:

**In classrooms:**

- Annotated work samples
- Drafts with reflections attached
- Whiteboards filled with crossed-out ideas (don't erase the process!)
- Voice recordings of students explaining their thinking

**In teams:**

- Decision logs that include *why*, not just *what*
- Strategy maps that show connections and tensions
- Shared documents that capture questions, not just answers
- Notes that include open questions alongside action items

Artifacts turn fleeting thinking into something collective and revisitable.

## 3. Value Process Language Out Loud

What we praise teaches people what counts. If we only celebrate speed, accuracy, and polish, people hide the work of thinking.

**Try naming:**

- "I noticed you revised your approach when that didn't work."
- "I appreciate how you tested two different strategies."
- "You changed your mind based on new information—that's strong thinking."
- "You asked a question that helped all of us see this differently."

**In teams:**

- "Thank you for naming your uncertainty."

- "That question slowed us down in a way we needed."
- "I'm glad you challenged that assumption."

When process language becomes normal, people stop protecting their thinking—and start sharing it.

## 4. Use Models—But Don't Let Them Replace Thinking

Frameworks, exemplars, and tools can clarify thinking. They can also constrain it.

The danger isn't the model. It's treating the model as the thinking itself.

**Try using models as:**

- Starting points (not endpoints)
- Conversation starters (not templates to copy)
- Tools to interrogate (not rules to follow)

**Ask:**

- "Where does this model help us?"
- "Where does it fall short?"
- "What doesn't fit?"
- "How might we adapt this for our context?"

Agency grows when people are allowed to think *with* tools—not submit to them.

## 5. Make Revision Visible—and Normal

If final work is the only work that's seen, learning freezes.

**Create space for:**

- Drafts

- False starts
- Changed minds
- Improved iterations

**Say things like:**

- "Show me how your thinking has evolved."
- "What would you revise if you had more time?"
- "What do you understand now that you didn't before?"
- "Where did you get stuck—and how did you move forward?"

Revision *isn't* remediation. It's evidence of learning.

## What This Might Look Like in Practice

### In a Grade 4 Math Classroom

**The situation:**

A teacher used to collect only final answers. She couldn't see *how* students were thinking.

**The shift:**

She asked students to submit three things:

1. Their first idea
2. Their revised strategy (if they changed approaches)
3. A brief reflection: "What shifted in your thinking?"

**The result:**

Students began talking about math differently. Mistakes became data. Strategies became shareable. Understanding deepened.

One student said: "I used to think math was about getting the right answer. Now I know it's about how you think."

### In a Secondary Science Class

**The situation:**

Lab reports followed rigid formats that prioritized procedure over thinking.

**The shift:**

Reports shifted to thinking-focused narratives:

- What were you expecting?
- What surprised you?
- How did the evidence change your thinking?
- What new questions emerged?

**The result:**

Scientific reasoning—not just following steps—came into focus. Students started thinking like scientists, not just performing experiments.

### In a School Leadership Team

**The situation:**

Major decisions were made, but the reasoning behind them often got lost. New leaders couldn't understand why certain things were done.

**The shift:**

The team added a simple practice: Every major decision included a visible *"thinking trail"*:

- What problem we were solving
- What options we considered
- Why we chose this path
- What we're still monitoring

**The result:**

Disagreements became easier to navigate. Trust increased. New leaders could enter conversations with context—not confusion.

## In a Nonprofit Organization

**The situation:**

After projects stalled repeatedly, a team realized they were documenting *tasks* but not *thinking*.

**The shift:**

They began ending project meetings with:

- "What's still unclear?"
- "What assumptions might we be making?"
- "What would we need to revisit if this doesn't work?"

**The result:**

Projects became more adaptive. Teams could course-correct earlier. The work felt more human—and more sustainable.

## Common Pitfalls (And How to Avoid Them)

### 1. Confusing Visibility with Accountability

This isn't about catching mistakes. It's about understanding thinking.

**What to try instead:** Frame it as learning: "What is this showing us?" not "Who got it wrong?"

### 2. Over-Scaffolding the Thinking

If every step is prescribed, there's nothing left to reveal. When learners follow a pre-digested process from start to finish, you see what they can execute—not what they actually understand. The scaffolding hides the thinking.

**What to try instead:** Give enough structure to start—then let thinking emerge organically.

### 3. Only Making Strong Thinking Visible

Learning lives in the partial and the tentative, too.

**What to try instead:** Celebrate struggle, revision, and half-formed ideas as much as polished thinking.

### 4. Treating Reflection as an Add-On

Thinking *is* the work—not the afterthought.

**What to try instead:** Build reflection into the flow, not just at the end.

### 5. Rushing to Clean Conclusions

Messy thinking is often the most generative. When we push too quickly toward tidy answers, we close down the very exploration that produces real understanding. Sitting with unresolved questions, even briefly, is where insight often lives.

**What to try instead:** Let ambiguity live a little longer. Not everything needs resolution immediately.

## Tiny Shift: Try This Tomorrow

Choose one moment where you usually look only at the result.

Add one prompt that reveals *thinking:*

- "How did you get there?"
- "What did you consider?"
- "What changed along the way?"
- "What surprised you?"

Capture the response—in writing, in conversation, on a shared board. Name its value: "This helps us see how you're thinking, not just what you produced."

Let others learn from it.

**Make the thinking visible—and then *let it matter.***

## Reflection Prompts

1. Where in your context is thinking currently invisible? What might that be costing?

2. What do people in your space feel safest showing: certainty or curiosity?

3. What artifacts currently capture conclusions but hide reasoning?

4. How do you respond when thinking is messy or incomplete? What message might that send?

5. What's one way you could publicly value *process*—not just outcomes—this week?

6. If thinking were more visible in your classroom, team, or organization, what might change?

## Closing Note

When thinking stays hidden, learning becomes fragile. When thinking is visible, learning becomes resilient.

**Agency grows when people see that their ideas—even unfinished ones—are worthy of attention.**

We don't need more polished products. We need clearer windows into how people think.

That's where learning strengthens. That's where agency takes root.

# CHAPTER 10

## SLOW DOWN TO SPEED UP

### Opening Scene

It's the end of a lesson. The teacher glances at the clock. *We need to move on.*

There's one more example to show. One more slide to advance. One more task to assign before the bell rings.

Students nod—not because they understand, but because the pace has taught them that confusion is something you carry quietly.

Later, during independent work, hands go up. Mistakes multiply. Frustration builds.

The lesson was "covered." *The learning wasn't.*

---

Now shift to a different room.

A project review meeting. The timeline is already tight. Everyone is behind, so the team skips reflection. They rush past questions. They decide quickly so they can move forward.

Weeks later, the same issues resurface. Rework piles up. Energy drains.

Someone finally says what everyone's thinking: "We keep moving fast but we're not actually getting anywhere."

---

Different contexts. Same pattern.

Speed feels productive. But unexamined speed often costs more time than it saves.

## Why This Matters

In nearly every environment—schools, nonprofits, corporate teams, leadership spaces—pace is treated as a proxy for effectiveness.

Fast meetings. Full agendas. Packed lessons. Rapid rollouts.

Slowness gets labeled as: Inefficient. Unfocused. Behind.

But learning—and good decision-making—doesn't happen at the speed of delivery. It happens at the speed of *sense-making*.

When pace outstrips understanding:

- People memorize instead of integrate
- Teams execute without alignment
- Mistakes repeat because no one paused to learn from them
- Burnout accelerates

Agency shrinks—sometimes so gradually that no one names it until it's gone. Because **agency requires time:**

Time to think.
Time to question.
Time to revisit.
Time to choose.

## The Tiny Shift

Here's the tiny shift at the heart of this chapter:

---

**FROM:** Rushing through (covering more)

**TO:** Building intentional pauses within the work (uncovering *meaning*)

---

Slowing down doesn't mean doing less. It means doing the right things long enough for them to stick.

When we slow down with purpose:

- Understanding deepens
- Decisions improve
- Execution accelerates (because fewer mistakes need fixing later)
- Energy returns

Paradoxically, **slowing down is often the fastest path forward.**

## How to Make This Shift

### 1. Build in Pause Points—On Purpose

Pauses don't happen accidentally. They have to be designed.

Try simple pause points:

**In lessons:**

- "Let's stop for 60 seconds—what's making sense so far?"
- "What's one thing you're still unsure about?"
- "Before we move on, what question should we answer together?"

**In meetings:**

- "Before we decide, what are we not considering yet?"

- "What would success require us to get right?"
- "Let's pause and make sure we're aligned before moving forward."

Pauses interrupt autopilot—and invite thinking back in.

### 2. Revisit Before You Add More

Many learning environments suffer from accumulation. We keep stacking new content, initiatives, or priorities on top of shaky foundations.

**Try revisiting:**

- "Where are we still unclear?"
- "What do we need to strengthen before moving forward?"
- "What assumption should we re-examine?"

**In classrooms:**

Return to a concept with a new lens. Compare strategies. Refine thinking.

**In teams:**

Revisit decisions. Adjust plans. Name what's changed.

**Revisiting *isn't* backtracking. It's consolidation.**

### 3. Replace Coverage with Depth

Coverage feels efficient. Depth is actually effective.

**Instead of asking:** "How much can we get through?"

**Ask:** "What's essential for people to truly understand?"

That might mean:

- Fewer learning objectives
- Shorter agendas
- Less content—but more meaning

Depth reduces re-teaching. It minimizes rework. It increases confidence and follow-through.

## 4. Build Reflection into the Flow (Not at the End)

Reflection is often treated as optional—or expendable when time runs out. But **reflection is where learning crystallizes.**

Try weaving it in:

**During work:**

- "What shifted in your thinking just now?"
- "What connections are you making?"
- "What surprised you?"

**After work:**

- "What will you do differently because of this?"
- "What did we learn from this experience?"
- "What would we repeat? What would we change next time?"

When reflection becomes routine, learning compounds.

## 5. Name the Purpose of Slowing Down

Slowing down can feel uncomfortable in fast-paced cultures. So name it.

**Say:**

- "We're slowing down here so we don't have to fix this later."
- "This pause is about clarity, not delay."
- "We're investing time now to save time later."

When people understand *why* the pace shifts, they're more willing to lean in.

## What This Might Look Like in Practice

### In an Elementary Classroom

**The situation:**

A teacher realized students could complete tasks but couldn't explain their thinking. They'd moved through content too quickly for understanding to stick.

**The shift:**

She added two minutes at the end of lessons:
"What's one thing you understand better now?"
"What's still confusing?"

**The result:**

Over time, confusion decreased. Independence increased. Learning sped up—because she'd slowed down enough for understanding to take root.

## In a Secondary School Department

**The situation:**

The team raced through units to "cover" curriculum. But students retained little.

**The shift:**

The department identified "non-negotiable understandings"—the concepts that mattered most. They slowed down there and moved faster elsewhere.

**The result:**

Assessment results improved. Student stress dropped. Teacher clarity increased. One teacher said: "We're teaching less—but students are learning more."

## In a Leadership Team

**The situation:**

A principal noticed decisions were being made quickly but revisited constantly—costing more time in the long run.

**The shift:**

The team introduced a standing question before finalizing anything:

"What would make this hard to undo? What do we need to get right?"

**The result:**

Decisions became more thoughtful—and more durable. The team moved slower upfront, but faster overall.

### In a Corporate L&D Program

**The situation:**

A leadership program packed dense content into every session. Participants left overwhelmed. Application was inconsistent.

**The shift:**

The facilitators replaced some content with reflection time. Participants spent time applying ideas to real challenges.

**The result:**

Implementation increased. Follow-up questions decreased. Impact deepened—because learning had time to land.

## Common Pitfalls (And How to Avoid Them)

### 1. Confusing Slowness with Lack of Urgency

Purposeful slowing is strategic—not passive.

**What to try instead:** Frame pauses as intentional investments, not delays.

### 2. Waiting Until Things Fall Apart to Slow Down

Proactive pauses prevent reactive fixes.

**What to try instead:** Build reflection into the rhythm before crises emerge.

### 3. Overloading Reflection with Paperwork

A single good question beats a long form.

**What to try instead:** Keep reflection simple and conversational.

### 4. Slowing Down Without Clarity

Pacing shifts need purpose.

**What to try instead:** Name why you're pausing. Help people see the value.

### 5. Trying to Do Everything Deeply

Depth requires prioritization.

**What to try instead:** Slow down for what matters most. Move efficiently through the rest.

## Tiny Shift: Try This Tomorrow

Identify one moment where things usually move too fast.

Insert a deliberate pause:

- One question
- One reflection
- One moment to check understanding

Say why you're doing it. Notice what changes.

Slow down just enough for *thinking* to catch up—and watch everything else speed up.

## Reflection Prompts

1. Where in your context does speed get rewarded over understanding?

2. What work keeps coming back because it was never fully understood the first time?

3. Where might a pause prevent future rework or confusion?

4. How do people respond when you slow the pace—relief or resistance? What might that tell you?

5. What's one area where depth could create more momentum than speed?

6. What might change if you gave people time to think—really think—before moving forward?

## Closing Note

Fast doesn't always mean forward. Busy doesn't always mean effective. When we slow down with intention, we honor how people actually learn and decide. We reduce friction. We build confidence. We create momentum that lasts.

**Agency doesn't grow in a rush. It grows in spaces where thinking has time to land.**

Often, the single most useful thing you can do is simply this: *Pause.*

# CHAPTER 11

## STRENGTH-SPOTTING AS A DAILY PRACTICE

### Opening Scene

A student hands in a piece of writing.

The teacher scans it quickly. The first thing she notices: *They still don't get paragraphing.*

Red pen out. Comments added. Next steps assigned.

The student reads the feedback and hears one message clearly: *I got it wrong again.*

---

Now shift the scene.

A manager listens to a team member describe a stalled project. The update ends with: "I'm not sure what to do next."

The manager responds:

"Have you tried being more organized?"
"Did you follow the process we set up?"
"What went wrong this time?"

The conversation ends politely. But something closes.

---

Different ages. Different contexts. Same outcome.

When feedback starts from deficits, people protect themselves. They comply. They withdraw. They stop taking risks.

**Agency erodes.**

## Why This Matters

Most systems are fluent in what's wrong.

We're trained to spot gaps: learning gaps, skill gaps, performance gaps. But constant deficit-spotting does more than identify problems.

**It shapes identity.**

Over time, people internalize the messages they hear most often:

"I'm behind."
"I'm not good at this."
"I need to be fixed."

That mindset erodes motivation. It narrows possibility. It makes agency feel unsafe.

Carol Dweck's research on growth mindset reveals that the language we use shapes how people see their own potential.[1] When we frame challenges as deficits to fix rather than capacities to grow, we inadvertently teach people that ability is fixed. But when we use language that assumes capability and names growth as ongoing, people develop resilience and agency.

**Strength-spotting doesn't ignore challenges. It changes the starting point.**

Because where we begin matters.

---

1. Dweck, C. (2006). *Mindset: The New Psychology of Success*. Random House.

## The Tiny Shift

Here's the tiny shift at the heart of this chapter:

---

**FROM:** Leading with what's missing (deficit-based language)
**TO:** Leading with what's already working (asset-based language)

---

Strength-spotting is not about praise. It's about *perception.*

It's the discipline of noticing capacity—even when performance is uneven.

It's choosing language that signals:

"I see your competence."
"I assume your capability."
"I believe growth is possible here."

**Those assumptions change everything.**

## How to Make This Shift

### 1. Practice Seeing Before Fixing

Before offering feedback, ask yourself:

- What is this person already doing well?
- What strengths are present but underutilized?
- What capabilities are emerging—even if imperfectly?

**In classrooms:**

- "You used evidence here in a powerful way."
- "I notice how you persisted through the tricky part."
- "You revised this section—that shows strong thinking."

**In teams:**

- "You clearly thought this through."
- "The way you anticipated that risk was smart."
- "I appreciate how you adapted when the plan changed."

**Seeing first doesn't eliminate next steps. It grounds them.**

## 2. Use Positive Presuppositions in Your Questions

The questions we ask reveal what we assume.

**Deficit-based questions sound like:**

- "Why didn't you … ?"
- "What went wrong?"
- "Where did you get stuck?"

**Positive presuppositions sound like:**

- "What strategies did you consider?"
- "What helped you make that decision?"
- "What's already working that we can build on?"
- "How did you manage to get this far?"

These questions assume thinking, intentionality, and capability. **People tend to rise to the assumptions placed upon them.**

## 3. Shift Feedback from Judgment to Discovery

Instead of evaluating, get curious.

**Try:**

- "Walk me through what you were aiming for."
- "What were you paying attention to here?"

- "What feels strongest to you in this work?"
- "What would you like to refine next?"

When feedback becomes a shared exploration, people stay open. **Agency stays intact.**

## 4. Normalize Growth Without Labeling Deficits

Growth doesn't require naming failure. It requires naming *possibility.*

**Replace:** "You're not ready yet."
**With:** "You're in the process of building this."

**Replace:** "This isn't strong."
**With:** "This part has potential—let's develop it."

**Replace:** "You need to improve … "
**With:** "What if you tried … ?"

Language that frames learning as ongoing keeps people engaged in the work.

## 5. Make Strength-Spotting a Daily Habit

Strength-spotting works best when it's consistent, not occasional.

Build it into routines:

- Open meetings by naming recent wins
- Invite students to reflect on strategies that worked
- Close conversations by identifying capabilities to leverage next time
- Publicly name when someone's contribution shifted the group's thinking

**When strength-spotting becomes cultural, confidence grows—quietly and steadily.**

## What This Might Look Like in Practice

### In an Early Years Classroom

**The situation:**

A teacher used to say "Good job!" to everything. It felt hollow.

**The shift:**

She started naming the actual strategy or strength:

"You found a way to solve that when it was hard."
"You asked for help when you needed it—that's a powerful strategy for learning."
"You kept trying even when it didn't work the first time."

**The result:**

Students began naming their own strategies instead of waiting for approval. They internalized: *I am capable.*

### In a Middle School Team

**The situation:**

Teachers gave feedback focused on fixing errors. Student revisions were minimal.

**The shift:**

They changed the feedback structure to: **"Build on this/Try next."**

Every piece of feedback started with what was working before suggesting next steps.

**The result:**

Student revisions improved. Ownership increased. Students felt capable—not broken.

## In a Nonprofit Organization

**The situation:**

Performance conversations focused on gaps and areas for improvement. Staff felt demoralized.

**The shift:**

A director reframed conversations around strengths:

"Where do you feel most effective?"
"What impact are you most proud of?"
"How can we build on what you're already doing well?"

**The result:**
Staff engagement increased. Turnover decreased. People felt seen—and capable.

## In Corporate Leadership Coaching

**The situation:**

Feedback conversations often felt evaluative and led to defensiveness.

**The shift:**

Leaders were coached to ask questions with positive presuppositions:

"What's working in how you're leading this?"
"What capability are you bringing that's making a difference?"
"How did you navigate that challenge?"

**The result:**

Conversations became more thoughtful. Defensiveness dropped. Problem-solving improved—because leaders were no longer protecting themselves from judgment. They were thinking alongside someone who assumed they were capable.

## Common Pitfalls (And How to Avoid Them)

### 1. Confusing Strength-Spotting with Flattery

This is about capability, not compliments. Flattery is vague and evaluative. It tells people you're pleased. Strength-spotting is specific and descriptive. It tells people what they're actually doing that's working. One builds dependence; the other builds agency.

**What to try instead:** Be specific. Name what you actually see.

### 2. Avoiding Hard Conversations

Strength-spotting doesn't replace accountability—it strengthens it. Naming what's working isn't a warm-up to the real conversation. It's the foundation that makes the real conversation possible.

**What to try instead:** Start with strengths, then address challenges honestly. The goal is growth, not false comfort.

### 3. Using Generic Praise

"Good job" doesn't help anyone grow. It names your reaction—not their capability. The more specific you are, the more useful the feedback becomes.

**What to try instead:** Name the specific strength, strategy, or thinking you notice.

### 4. Only Naming Strengths When Things Go Well

Growth moments matter most. When we only notice strengths in moments of success, we inadvertently teach people that capability is conditional—something they have when things go right, not something they carry into difficulty.

**What to try instead:** Notice strengths even when outcomes aren't perfect.

### 5. Assuming People Know Their Strengths Already

Many don't—until someone names them. People often discount their own capabilities or assume what comes naturally to them is ordinary. Naming it out loud makes it real.

**What to try instead:** Make strengths visible and explicit.

## Tiny Shift: Try This Tomorrow

In your next conversation—lesson debrief, coaching session, team check-in—start here: **Name one strength you genuinely observe.**

Then ask one question that assumes capability:

- "What's working here that we can build on?"
- "What strength are you bringing to this?"

Invite one next step that builds forward—not backward. Notice how the energy shifts.

## Reflection Prompts

1. What do people in your context hear more often: what's wrong or what's possible?

2. How might your questions reveal hidden assumptions about capability?

3. Where could positive presuppositions unlock deeper thinking or engagement?

4. When have you felt most motivated by someone naming your strengths? What did that create?

5. What could change if strength-spotting became a daily practice—not an occasional gesture?

6. How do you currently respond when someone struggles? What message might that send about what you value?

## Closing Note

People grow in the direction of what we notice. When we lead with deficits, we get compliance—and often, resignation. When we lead with strengths, we invite agency.

**Strength-spotting is not soft. It's strategic.** It's how we build confidence without arrogance. Capability without pressure. Growth without fear.

When people feel seen for what they *can do,* they're far more willing to discover what they *might do next.*

**That's how agency takes root.**

---

With these daily moves—designing together, building safe routines, asking better questions, making thinking visible, slowing down, and spotting strengths—we create the conditions where agency becomes not just possible, but expected.

These aren't one-time strategies. They're rhythms. Habits. Ways of being with learners, teams, and ourselves. When they compound over time, they *transform* culture.

Now let's turn to leadership—because sustaining these moves requires more than individual practice. It requires leaders who create the conditions where agency can breathe.

# PART THREE
# LEADING FOR AGENCY
## CREATING CULTURES WHERE PEOPLE CAN LEARN, LEAD, AND THRIVE

The daily moves in Part II are vital. They're the habits that make agency real.

But those moves don't sustain themselves. They need protection. They need support. They need leaders who understand that their job isn't to create agency *in* people—it's to create the conditions where agency can flourish.

This section is about leadership—not as position or title, but as the work of shaping culture, protecting what matters, and trusting people with more than we're comfortable trusting them with.

If you're a classroom teacher, you're a leader. If you're a coach or facilitator, you're a leader. If you hold a formal leadership role, this is your work. Leadership, as this section uses the word, is any act of shaping the conditions others work and learn within. That's a wide net—and it's meant to be.

Let's explore what it means to lead *for* agency—not just talk about it.

# CHAPTER 12

## PROTECTING TIME, ENERGY, AND FOCUS

### Opening Scene

It's 9:47 AM on a Tuesday. A product manager opens her laptop to finally tackle the strategic planning document she's been putting off all week. She blocks two hours on her calendar. Closes Slack. Puts her phone face-down.

Three minutes in, a meeting invite appears for 10:30. Someone messages: "Quick question?" A notification reminds her about the report due Friday.

She tries to refocus. Reads the same paragraph three times.

Another ping. Her calendar now shows six meetings today, with thirty- to forty-minute gaps between them—just enough time to feel fragmented, not enough to think deeply about anything.

By 4 PM, she's attended five meetings, sent forty-three messages, and made exactly zero progress on the work that actually matters.

She's exhausted. But she can't point to anything meaningful she's produced.

Now shift the scene.

A teacher sits down to plan during her only free period. She's been thinking about tomorrow's lesson all day—turning ideas over in her head while monitoring recess, eating lunch standing up, responding to three urgent emails.

She has thirty minutes.

Her inbox pings. A meeting reminder pops up. A student knocks on the door needing to make up a quiz.

By the time she opens her planner, she has twelve minutes left. Her brain is scattered. The planning she manages feels rushed, shallow—not the thoughtful design she wanted.

---

Different roles. Different settings. Same underlying problem.

Time is being spent. Energy is being drained. Focus is being fragmented. **No amount of motivation can compensate for conditions that make meaningful work nearly impossible.**

Cal Newport's research on deep work shows that fragmented attention dramatically reduces the quality of thinking and decision-making.[1] When we context-switch constantly—from email to meeting to task to interruption—our cognitive capacity diminishes. We're busy, but we're not productive. We're moving, but we're not learning.

## Why This Matters

Agency doesn't survive in chaos. When people are constantly interrupted, overloaded, and pulled in competing directions, the nervous system goes into survival mode.

In survival mode:

- People comply
- They rush

1. Newport, C. (2016). *Deep Work: Rules for Focused Success in a Distracted World.* Grand Central Publishing.

- They do what's loudest or most urgent
- They stop thinking deeply

This isn't a personal failing. It's a *design* problem.

Leaders often talk about resilience, ownership, and initiative. But those qualities can't flourish when time is scarce, energy is depleted, and focus is fractured.

Agency requires:

- Protected time to think
- Sustainable energy
- Clear priorities
- Boundaries that signal what matters

Protecting these *isn't* a "nice to have." It's a *leadership responsibility.*

## The Tiny Shift

Here's the tiny shift at the heart of this chapter:

---

**FROM:** Managing people's output: *"How do we get more done?"*

**TO:** Protecting the conditions that make good work possible: *"What deserves our best thinking—and what needs to stop competing for it?"*

---

Leadership that supports agency isn't about pushing harder. It's about clearing space.

When leaders protect time, energy, and focus:

- People make better decisions
- Learning deepens
- Initiative increases
- Burnout decreases
- Less truly becomes better

## How to Make This Shift

### 1. Treat Time as a Collective Resource

Time doesn't belong only to individuals. It's a shared asset.

When leaders overload calendars, schedule back-to-back meetings, or treat every request as urgent, they unintentionally teach: *Your time isn't yours to protect.*

**Try asking:**

- "What deserves uninterrupted time?"
- "What meetings actually need to exist?"
- "What could be asynchronous instead of synchronous?"

**Protect blocks for:**

- Planning and preparation
- Deep work
- Genuine collaboration (not just updates)
- Reflection

When leaders model time protection, others follow.

### 2. Design Meetings That Respect Energy

Meetings are one of the biggest drains on agency.

**Common problems:** Too many. Too long. Too unfocused. Too performative.

**Shift meeting design by:**

- Clarifying purpose: "Is this for decisions, learning, or updates?"

- Sharing information ahead of time (don't use precious time for announcements)
- Reducing length (45 minutes instead of 60; 25 instead of 30)
- Ending early when possible
- Building in pause points for thinking

**Ask:** *"If this meeting disappeared, what would actually break?"*

Often, the answer is: very little.

## 3. Limit the Number of Priorities (Seriously)

When everything is a priority, nothing is. **Agency thrives on clarity.**

**People need to know:**

- What matters most
- What can wait
- What's off the table

**Leaders build agency when they:**

- Name 1-3 true priorities
- Revisit them regularly
- Say "not now" to competing initiatives
- Protect those priorities fiercely

This isn't about lack of ambition. It's about focus.

## 4. Protect Energy, Not Just Time

Time can be scheduled. Energy needs to be stewarded.

**Notice:**

- Where are people most depleted?

- Where are demands emotionally heavy?
- Where are transitions constant?

**Small shifts help:**

- No-meeting days or half-days
- Buffer time between meetings
- Rotating high-demand responsibilities
- Honest conversations about capacity

Energy is not infinite. Treating it as such erodes trust.

### 5. Model "Less but Better"

What leaders tolerate becomes culture. If leaders respond instantly to everything, fill every gap with more activity, and work constantly, others will too.

**Model:**

- Boundaries around work time
- Rest and recovery
- Focused attention on what matters
- Intentional slowing

Not as a performance. *As a practice.* Agency grows when people see that doing less—well—is valued.

## What This Might Look Like in Practice

### In a Primary School

**The situation:**

A principal noticed teachers had almost no uninterrupted planning time. Meetings filled every gap. Teachers were exhausted, planning happened at home, and lesson quality was suffering.

**The shift:**

She restructured the schedule:

- **Protected weekly planning blocks:** 90 minutes every Thursday afternoon, sacred and non-negotiable
- **Reduced staff meetings:** From weekly to bi-weekly, with agendas limited to decisions only
- **Clear boundaries:** "Emergencies" were defined (student safety, family crisis). Everything else could wait.
- **Asynchronous updates:** School announcements moved to a weekly email digest

Teachers now had time to actually plan—together or alone—without interruptions.

**The result:**

Planning quality improved dramatically. Teachers started collaborating during protected time instead of working in isolation at home. Morale lifted. One teacher said: "I finally feel like I can think about my teaching instead of just surviving it."

Most importantly: instruction strengthened because teachers had space to design meaningful learning experiences.

### In a Secondary School

**The situation:**

Department meetings ran 60-75 minutes and felt like a waste of time. Most of the agenda was announcements and updates that could have been emails. Teachers left drained, not energized.

**The shift:**

The department head redesigned meetings entirely:

- **Asynchronous information sharing:** Created a weekly "Department Digest" with updates, resources, and announcements—sent Friday afternoons
- **Meeting purpose redefined:** Meetings now reserved exclusively for collaborative problem-solving and decision-making
- **40-minute cap:** Meetings started on time, ended on time, no exceptions
- **Always ended 5 minutes early:** Built in transition time before next commitments

When meetings did happen, the agenda was simple: "What decision do we need to make together? What problem are we trying to solve?"

**The result:**

Teachers actually looked forward to meetings. One said: "I stopped dreading these meetings. My thinking is needed—not just my attendance. That's not a small thing." Collaboration deepened. Energy shifted from resentment to genuine engagement.

### In a Nonprofit Organization

**The situation:**

Staff were juggling five major initiatives simultaneously: a new program launch, grant reporting, community outreach expansion, internal systems overhaul, and board development. Nothing got the focused attention it deserved. People were exhausted and frustrated.

**The shift:**

Leadership made a difficult but necessary choice: they named **three priorities for the year**—and formally paused the other two until the following year.

The three priorities:

1. Launch the new program well (not just fast)
2. Strengthen community relationships (not just expand reach)
3. Complete grant requirements with integrity (not just compliance)

Everything else was explicitly put on hold. When new opportunities arose, leadership asked: "Does this serve one of our three priorities? If not, we say 'not now.'"

**The result:**

Staff stopped context-switching constantly. The work they did do, they did deeply and well. One team member said: "For years, I'd been moving fast and going nowhere. Now we're actually landing things."

Impact increased because focus returned. Burnout decreased. The work felt sustainable again.

## In a Corporate Team

**The situation:**

A product team was in back-to-back meetings from 9 AM to 5 PM most days. Deep work happened at night or on weekends. Quality suffered. People were burned out. One engineer said: "I can't remember the last time I had two hours to actually think."

**The shift:**

The manager implemented **"focus mornings"**—no meetings before noon on Tuesdays and Thursdays.

She communicated it clearly to stakeholders: "This team needs uninterrupted time to do the work you're asking them to do. We're protecting focus time so we can deliver better results."

She also modeled it herself—blocking her own calendar and declining morning meeting requests on those days.

**The result:**

Deep work returned. One developer said: "I can finally get into flow state again. I'm solving problems I've been stuck on for weeks."

Product quality measurably improved. Bugs decreased. Innovation increased. Most importantly, people stopped working nights and weekends just to catch up on thinking work.

Trust deepened because the manager protected what mattered instead of just talking about it.

## Common Pitfalls (And How to Avoid Them)

### 1. Confusing Urgency with Importance

Loud doesn't mean critical. Urgent requests tend to crowd out important work—not because they matter more, but because they're louder and more immediate.

**What to try instead:** Distinguish between what's urgent and what actually matters. Protect the important.

### 2. Protecting Leaders' Time but Not Others'

Equity matters. When only those at the top get protected thinking time, the message sent—however unintentionally—is that their thinking matters more.

**What to try instead:** If time protection is valuable for leaders, it's valuable for everyone. Audit whose calendar is most fragmented. That's often where the biggest gains are.

### 3. Adding New Priorities Without Removing Old Ones

This breaks trust. When leaders add without subtracting, people learn that priorities are just intentions—not real commitments. The list grows, focus fractures, and the newest "priority" gets the same fate as the last one: acknowledged, then quietly buried under everything else.

**What to try instead:** Every time you add something, name what you're removing or pausing.

### 4. Treating Exhaustion as a Motivation Problem

It's usually a systems problem. When people are depleted, the instinct is often to inspire them: a pep talk, a retreat, a renewed sense of purpose. But if the meeting load, the initiative count, or the expectation of constant availability hasn't changed, the energy won't either.

**What to try instead:** Look at conditions, not character. What's draining energy unnecessarily?

### 5. Assuming People Will Protect Their Own Time Without Permission

They won't—unless leaders do first. If the culture treats boundary-setting as laziness or lack of dedication, people will sacrifice their thinking time before they sacrifice their reputation.

**What to try instead:** Model it. Name it. Protect it systematically.

## Tiny Shift: Try This Tomorrow

Look at your calendar—or your team's calendar.

Circle one thing that drains time or energy without meaningful return. Remove it. Or redesign it.

Then protect one block of time for deep, meaningful work.

Name it. Defend it. *Notice what changes.*

## Reflection Prompts

1. Where is time currently being spent in your context—but value isn't being created?
2. What interrupts focus most often? What might it take to reduce those interruptions?
3. Which meetings could be redesigned—or removed entirely?
4. What priorities need clearer boundaries to protect them?
5. How might your own behavior model what's acceptable around time and energy? What message might that send?
6. If you could give people one gift related to time, energy, or focus, what would it be?

## Closing Note

Agency doesn't thrive on hustle. It thrives on care. When leaders protect time, energy, and focus, they send a powerful message:

*Your thinking matters. Your well-being matters. This work matters.*

When those conditions are in place, people don't need to be pushed. They're finally free to do their best work.

**That's what leading for agency looks like.**

# CHAPTER 13

## FEEDBACK THAT GROWS PEOPLE, NOT PRESSURE

### Opening Scene

A student gets a paper back. The grade is circled. A few comments sit in the margins:

"Be clearer."
"Needs more detail."
"Watch your organization."

The student skims it, shrugs, and stuffs it into a backpack.
Nothing changes.

---

Now shift the scene.

An employee finishes a performance review. The manager has done their homework. The feedback is honest. The expectations are clear.

But afterward, the employee tells a colleague: "I know what I did wrong ... I just don't know what to do next."

Different contexts. Same result.

**Feedback was given. Learning didn't happen.**

Because feedback that judges performance without growing capability doesn't build agency. It builds pressure.

## Why This Matters

Most people want feedback. They just don't want evaluation masquerading as support.

In many systems, feedback has become:

- A verdict
- A ranking
- A justification for decisions already made

Even when it's well-intentioned, it often lands as:

"You're being measured."
"You're being compared."
"You're being corrected."

That activates defensiveness, and defensiveness shuts down learning. Agency requires something different.

**Agency grows when feedback:**

- Clarifies purpose
- Builds on strengths
- Names next steps with precision
- Assumes capability
- Points forward

In other words: feedback that grows people doesn't just look back. **It feeds forward.**[1]

## The Tiny Shift

Here's the tiny shift at the heart of this chapter:

---

**FROM:** Feedback as evaluation: *"What went wrong?"*
**TO:** Feedback as a learning conversation: *"Where are we going, where are you now, and what's the most useful next move?"*

---

This is where the interplay of feed up, feed back, and feed forward matters:

- **Feed up** clarifies the destination: *What are we aiming for? What might success look like?*
- **Feed back** reflects the present: *What's happening now? What's working? What patterns do we see?*
- **Feed forward** shapes growth: *What's the next step? What might you try? What could move this forward?*

When all three are present, feedback becomes a bridge—not a judgment.

## How to Make This Shift

### 1. Start with Feed Up: Reconnect to Purpose

Feedback without direction feels arbitrary.

---

1. This concept draws on the work of John Hattie and Helen Timperley. See Hattie, J. & Timperley, H. (2007). "The Power of Feedback," *Review of Educational Research*, 77(1), 81-112. They outline feedback as operating at three levels: feed up (Where am I going?), feed back (How am I going?), and feed forward (Where to next?).

Before offering suggestions, ground the conversation in shared clarity:

- "What are we working toward here?"
- "What does quality look like in this context?"
- "What matters most in this moment?"

**In classrooms:**

"This piece is about helping the reader follow your thinking clearly."

**In teams:**

"This project is meant to improve response time for customers while maintaining quality."

Feed up gives feedback *a reason to exist.*

## 2. Use Feedback to Grow Strengths—Not Just Fix Gaps

Most feedback cultures default to deficit-spotting. But growth accelerates when we expand what's already working.

**Try naming:**

- "I notice how you ... "
- "This part is strong because ... "
- "The way you approached X is helping Y."

This isn't flattery. It's *usable data.* When people understand *why* something works, they can do it again—on purpose.

## 3. Make Feed Forward Specific Enough to Transfer

Vague advice creates pressure. Specific guidance creates possibility. This is where what I call the ***Transfer Equation*** matters:

**What + How + Why**
or, in other words:
**Skill + Strategy + Relevance**

Here's why all three components are essential: Too often, we give people the *What* without the *How* or *Why*—and then wonder why nothing changes.

"Use evidence to support your claim."
"Be more organized."
"Take more initiative."

These sound like feedback. But they're not actionable. They name a destination without showing the path.

The ***Transfer Equation*** ensures feedback actually transfers into practice.

**Example:**

- **What:** "Writers use evidence to support their claims."
- **How:** "One way you can do this is to first embed a quote, and then explain *how it connects* to your point."
- **Why:** "This is important because it helps readers follow your reasoning without having to guess."

Without all three, feedback doesn't transfer. With all three, people can act.

## 4. Ask Questions That Assume Capability

Instead of telling people what to do, invite reflection with questions that presuppose competence:

- "What led you to make that choice?"
- "What strategies were you drawing on here?"
- "What might you build on next?"
- "What feels like the strongest leverage point for growth?"

These questions keep ownership with the learner. They invite thinking. *They strengthen agency.*

### 5. Keep Feedback Dialogic, Not Performative

Feedback should be something people *use,* not something they endure.

**Try closing conversations with:**

- "What part of this feels most useful right now?"
- "What would you like to try next?"
- "What support would help you move forward?"

When feedback becomes dialogue, pressure decreases—and learning increases.

## What This Might Look Like in Practice

### In an Upper Elementary Classroom

**The situation:**

A teacher used to mark everything wrong on student writing. Students felt overwhelmed and didn't revise.

**The shift:**

She highlighted one writing strength and named one next step—clearly connected, and specific enough to transfer.

For example: "Your lead grabs the reader's attention—starting with what the character is thinking makes us feel like we're right there with him. Try doing that same thing in your second paragraph, but this time through what he says or does. When we see a character act instead of being told how he feels, we get to figure it out ourselves—and that's what keeps readers hooked."

**The result:**

Students revised more thoughtfully. Transfer improved. They felt capable, not defeated.

## In a Secondary School

**The situation:**

Post-observation feedback felt evaluative. Teachers left defensive, not empowered.

**The shift:**

Department leaders shifted to **feed up, feed back, and feed forward** conversations:

- Feed up: "We're working toward students doing more of the thinking."
- Feed back: "Students were clearly engaged; there was real energy in the room, and they wanted to participate. What I noticed is that most of the questions were flowing through you, so the cognitive work was still largely yours."
- Feed forward: "What if you tried posing the question and then giving 60 seconds of silent think time before anyone responds? That pause might be all they need to do more of the heavy lifting."

**The result:**

Teacher trust increased. Instruction improved. Feedback felt like partnership, not judgment.

## In a Coaching Conversation

**The situation:**

A coach used to jump straight to suggestions—well-intentioned ones, but suggestions nonetheless. Teachers left with strategies they hadn't asked for and felt little ownership over.

**The shift:**

The coach started with: "What's one move you're proud of in that lesson?"

Then: "What might you build on next time?"

**The result:**

Teachers stayed open. Growth felt owned, not assigned. The coaching relationship deepened—because the teacher's thinking was driving it, not the coach's.

## In a Corporate Setting

**The situation:**

Performance reviews felt like report cards. People left knowing they fell short, but not knowing how to grow.

**The shift:**

Managers trained in feed forward conversations. Reviews became:

- "Here's what you're doing well and why it's working."
- "Here's where I see opportunity for growth."
- "Here's one specific thing to try next quarter—and why it matters."

**The result:**

People left with clarity—not shame. They knew what was working, why it mattered, and exactly what to try next. Performance improved because feedback became actionable—and because people actually *wanted* to act on it.

## Common Pitfalls (And How to Avoid Them)

### 1. Giving Feedback Without Clear Purpose

Feed up matters. Without it, feedback feels random—even when it's accurate. People need to know what they're working toward before they can make sense of where they are in relation to it. Feedback without direction is just commentary.

**What to try instead:** Consistently start with "where we're headed."

### 2. Focusing Only on What's Wrong

Growth comes from leverage, not just repair.

**What to try instead:** Name strengths with the same specificity you name next steps.

### 3. Offering Vague Next Steps

"Be better" doesn't help anyone. Vague next steps create pressure without direction; people know they've fallen short but have no clear path forward.

**What to try instead:** Use the What + How + Why structure. Make it transferable.

### 4. Overloading People with Too Much Feedback

Five suggestions feel overwhelming. When people can't decide where to start, they often don't start anywhere.

**What to try instead:** One good, actionable next move beats a laundry list.

### 5. Confusing Feedback with Fixing

Agency stays with the learner when feedback invites thinking, not compliance. When we fix things for people—rewriting their draft, solving their problem, prescribing their next move—we get short-term improvement and long-term dependence. The goal isn't a better product. It's a more capable person.

**What to try instead:** Ask questions. Invite partnership. Trust capability.

## Tiny Shift: Try This Tomorrow

In your next feedback conversation:

1. **Clarify the goal** (feed up): "Here's what we're working toward. What matters most to you in this work?"
2. **Name one strength** that's working (feed back).
3. **Offer one specific next step** using the ***Transfer Equation:*** What + How + Why (feed forward).

Watch how the tone—and impact—shift.

## Reflection Prompts

1. How does feedback currently feel in your context—supportive or stressful?

2. Which part do you emphasize most: feed up, feed back, or feed forward? What might you be missing?

3. How specific is the feedback people receive? Can they actually act on it?

4. Where might positive presuppositions (assuming capability) change the conversation?

5. How often does feedback in your context lead to clear, next-step action? What could increase that?

6. What could shift if feedback felt more like partnership and less like evaluation?

## Closing Note

Feedback should feel like an invitation—not a verdict. When we shift from evaluation to growth, pressure decreases, learning deepens, and agency expands.

People don't grow because they're told what's wrong. They grow when they're shown *what's possible*—and supported in getting there.

That's feedback that feeds forward.

**That's how leaders grow people, not pressure.**

# CHAPTER 14

## BUILDING COMMUNITIES OF PRACTICE

### Opening Scene

It's late afternoon in a school. A teacher closes her classroom door and exhales. She's been working hard all day. Trying new strategies. Responding to student needs. Adjusting on the fly.

But she feels alone with it all.

Down the hall, another teacher is wrestling with the exact same challenges.

They pass each other in the parking lot. Smile. Wave. Drive home separately. Both carrying the weight alone.

---

Now shift the scene.

A team of professionals in a growing organization. Everyone is competent. Everyone is busy. Everyone is responsible for their own outcomes.

They attend the same meetings. They share the same goals.

But their actual learning happens in isolation.

When problems arise, people search online. They improvise. They quietly reinvent wheels that others have already built.

---

Different contexts. Same pattern.

**When learning lives only inside individuals, growth is fragile.**

**When learning lives between people, it compounds.**

## Why This Matters

We often treat learning as a private act: Your classroom. Your caseload. Your role. Your performance. But expertise doesn't actually grow that way.

Research across education, organizational learning, and professional development tells a consistent story: **People get better when they learn with others.**[1]

Communities of practice—whether they're called PLCs, learning circles, peer coaching groups, or professional networks—work because they shift learning from individual effort to collective sense-making.

And that shift matters for agency.

Agency doesn't just require confidence. It requires:

- Language to name practice
- Peers to test ideas with
- Shared norms that make risk-taking safe
- Structures that sustain learning over time

Without community, agency becomes exhausting. With community, it becomes sustainable.

1. For foundational work on communities of practice, see Wenger, E. (1998). *Communities of Practice: Learning, Meaning, and Identity*. Cambridge University Press.

## The Tiny Shift

Here's the tiny shift at the heart of this chapter:

---

**FROM:** Seeing professional learning as something individuals do: *"Everyone improve your own practice."*

**TO:** Seeing it as something communities build together: *"How can we learn, reflect, and grow—collectively?"*

---

Communities of practice don't remove individual responsibility. They multiply it. When people learn together, they:

- Normalize struggle
- Spread expertise
- Reduce isolation
- Increase coherence
- Sustain momentum

**Agency becomes less about personal grit—and more about shared growth.**

## How to Make This Shift

### 1. Anchor Communities in Real Practice

Communities of practice fail when they drift into abstraction. They succeed when they focus on:

- Real work
- Real dilemmas
- Real learners, clients, or teams

**Try grounding conversations in:**

- Student work
- Lesson artifacts
- Case studies from actual projects
- Live challenges teams are facing
- Decision points people are navigating right now

The question shifts from: *"What should we be doing?"*
To: *"What's happening—and how do we make sense of it together?"*

## 2. Create Predictable Structures That Hold the Learning

Connection alone isn't enough. Communities need structure.

**Effective communities often rely on:**

- Regular meeting rhythms (same time, same place, predictable)
- Clear purposes for each gathering (Are we learning together? Problem-solving? Sharing resources?)
- Simple protocols for discussion (rounds, tuning, consultancy)
- Agreed-upon norms for listening, challenge, and support

Structure doesn't limit conversation. **It protects it.** It ensures that everyone has voice, thinking is visible, and time is used well.

## 3. Use Peer Coaching to Grow Agency, Not Dependence

Peer coaching works when it's about thinking—not fixing. Instead of advice-giving, try coaching moves like:

- "What are you noticing?"

- "What feels most challenging here?"
- "What options are you considering?"
- "What support would be most useful right now?"

These questions keep ownership with the person closest to the work. **Peer coaching isn't about having the best answers. It's about helping each other ask better questions.**

### 4. Build Shared Language for Practice

Communities grow stronger when they develop common language.

Shared language helps people:

- Name strategies more precisely
- Talk about impact with clarity
- Reflect more efficiently
- Learn faster together

This might include:

- Agreed-upon instructional practices
- Common planning templates or frameworks
- Shared feedback language
- Collective definitions of quality

When language is shared, learning accelerates—and agency expands.

### 5. Protect the Community from Becoming Another Task

One of the fastest ways to kill a community of practice is to overload it.

Avoid turning it into:

- A compliance checklist
- An accountability report

- Another meeting to survive

Instead, protect it as:

- A learning space
- A thinking space
- A relational space

Ask regularly:

- "What's actually helping us grow?"
- "What feels performative?"
- "What do we need to adjust?"

Communities thrive when they remain useful—not when they become mandatory drudgery.

## What This Might Look Like in Practice

### In a Primary School PLC

**The situation:**

Teams used to bring lesson plans to meetings and talk through what they'd teach. Conversations stayed surface-level—pleasant, but rarely changing what happened in classrooms.

**The shift:**

They started bringing student work instead—actual artifacts showing student thinking.

They analyzed together: "What does this tell us about what students understand? What might they be ready for next?"

**The result:**

Instruction aligned naturally because teachers were responding to the same evidence. Confidence grew across the team. Teachers felt less alone—and more like professionals making informed decisions together.

## In a Secondary Department

**The situation:**

Department meetings felt dominated by a few voices. Quieter teachers rarely contributed—not because they had nothing to say, but because the structure never made space for them.

**The shift:**

Teachers rotated facilitation roles. Protocols ensured equitable voice —everyone contributed before anyone elaborated..

**The result:**

Professional dialogue deepened. Leadership became shared across the group, not concentrated in one person. Over time, teachers who had been silent started shaping the direction of the department's work.

## In a Nonprofit Organization

**The situation:**

Staff felt isolated in their work. When challenges arose, people struggled alone: searching for solutions online, improvising, and quietly assuming everyone else had it figured out.

**The shift:**

They formed learning circles around real challenges. Each session began with someone naming a genuine dilemma from their work.

Peer coaching replaced top-down problem-solving. The role of the group was to ask better questions, not supply quick answers.

**The result:**

Innovation increased. Burnout decreased. People felt supported—not because someone above them had fixed things, but because they were no longer carrying the work alone.

## In a Corporate Environment

**The situation:**

Learning happened in silos. Teams didn't know what other teams were discovering—which meant problems got solved repeatedly, and hard-won insights disappeared the moment a project ended.

**The shift:**

Cross-functional communities met monthly to reflect on practice and share insights. Each gathering centered on a real question, not a status update: *"What have you learned recently that surprised you? What are you still figuring out?"*

**The result:**

People learned beyond their departments. Capability spread faster than formal training ever achieved—because the knowledge already existed in the room, and the community gave it somewhere to go.

## Common Pitfalls (And How to Avoid Them)

### 1. Confusing Community with Collegiality

Nice conversations don't automatically lead to learning. When a community stays at the level of sharing updates and affirming each other, it can feel connected without ever actually building collective knowledge.

**What to try instead:** Ground conversations in real practice. Make thinking visible.

### 2. Letting One or Two Voices Dominate

Agency requires distributed participation. When the same voices drive every conversation, others learn to wait—and the community loses the perspectives it most needs to hear.

**What to try instead:** Use structures that spread voice. Rotate roles.

### 3. Over-Structuring the Work

Too many protocols suffocate learning. When every conversation follows a rigid format, people spend their energy navigating the process instead of engaging with the ideas.

**What to try instead:** Use just enough structure to hold the thinking. Stay flexible.

### 4. Under-Structuring the Work

Too little structure leads to drift and frustration. Without a clear purpose or a simple protocol to organize the conversation, communities often default to the path of least resistance—which is usually just talking.

**What to try instead:** Name purposes, use simple protocols, create predictability.

### 5. Treating Communities as Temporary

Growth needs continuity. Trust between colleagues takes time to build. The kind of honest, vulnerable conversation that drives real learning doesn't happen in a one-time workshop or a six-week cohort. When communities disband before that trust forms, people return to working in isolation, often feeling like the whole effort wasn't worth it.

**What to try instead:** Commit long-term. Let relationships and trust build over time.

## Tiny Shift: Try This Tomorrow

Identify one group you're already part of.

Add one small move:

- Bring a real artifact from practice (student work, project example, dilemma)
- Ask one coaching question instead of offering advice
- Name one pattern you're noticing in your own work

Shift the conversation from sharing updates *to making meaning together.* That's how communities of practice begin to take root.

## Reflection Prompts

1. Where do people currently learn alone when they could learn together?

2. What structures already exist that could become communities of practice?

3. How safe does it feel to share unfinished thinking in your context?

4. What language do people use to talk about practice—and what's missing?

5. What might sustainable, collective growth look like in your setting?

## Closing Note

Learning is not meant to be a solo act.

When we create communities of practice, we move learning out of isolation and into relationship. We make growth visible. We distribute expertise. We sustain momentum even when things get hard.

**Agency doesn't just live inside individuals. It lives in the spaces where people think, struggle, and grow—together.**

When those spaces are intentionally designed, learning doesn't fade when pressure rises. It deepens.

That's the power of community.

# CHAPTER 15

## LEADING THROUGH TRUST, NOT CONTROL

### Opening Scene

A leader stands at the front of the room. The agenda is set. The outcomes are clear. The expectations have been communicated.

People listen. They comply. They do what's asked. From the outside, it looks like strong leadership.

But beneath the surface, something else is happening. Questions stay unasked. Concerns go unspoken. Ideas remain half-formed. Energy is cautious, not committed.

---

Now shift the scene.

A different leader opens a meeting with: "Here's what we're trying to accomplish. Here's what I'm holding as non-negotiable. And here's where I need your thinking."

The room feels different.

People lean in. They challenge assumptions. They name risks early.

They offer ideas. They take responsibility—not because they're told to, but because the work genuinely belongs to them too.

---

Different approaches. Different outcomes.

The difference isn't personality. It isn't charisma. It isn't even experience. **It's trust.**

## Why This Matters

Control is often mistaken for leadership. Especially in high-stakes environments—schools, organizations, nonprofits, systems under pressure—control can feel responsible. It promises predictability. It reduces uncertainty. It creates the illusion of safety. But control comes with a hidden cost.

**When leaders hold all the decisions:**

- Others stop thinking ahead
- Others wait for direction
- Others protect themselves instead of contributing fully
- Initiative dies
- Innovation stalls
- Agency withers

Trust doesn't mean anything goes. It doesn't mean standards disappear. It doesn't mean leaders abdicate responsibility.

**Trust means something more demanding:** Believing—deeply and consistently—that people are capable of thinking, learning, and contributing meaningfully when the conditions are right. And then creating those conditions.

Research on high-performing teams consistently shows that trust is the foundation of everything else—collaboration, innovation, accountability, and results.[1] Without trust, even the most skilled teams underperform. With it, ordinary groups achieve extraordinary things.

## The Tiny Shift

Here's the tiny shift at the heart of this chapter:

---

**FROM:** Leading through control
**TO:** Leading through trust

---

**Control asks:** "How do I make sure this goes the way I want?"

**Trust asks:** "How do I create the conditions for good judgment to emerge—beyond me?"

Control centralizes power. Trust distributes it—intentionally.

Control relies on compliance. Trust relies on commitment.

**And commitment is where agency lives.**

## How to Make This Shift

### 1. Be Clear About What Isn't Up for Negotiation

Trust does not mean vagueness. In fact, trust grows fastest when constraints are transparent.

Name:

- The purpose (why we're doing this)
- The non-negotiables (what must be true)
- The responsibilities you still hold as a leader

Say things like:

1. Lencioni, P. (2002). *The Five Dysfunctions of a Team: A Leadership Fable.* Jossey-Bass. Lencioni identifies trust as the foundational layer upon which all other team dynamics rest—without it, teams cannot engage in productive conflict, commit to decisions, hold each other accountable, or focus on collective results.

- "Here's what we must accomplish."
- "Here's what I'm accountable for."
- "Here's where we have flexibility."

Clarity is not control. It's a gift. It lets people know where they can innovate safely.

### 2. Share Power Where It Actually Matters

Token choice erodes trust. Real influence builds it.

Ask yourself:

- Where do decisions genuinely affect people's work?
- Where is local knowledge stronger than positional authority?
- Where does ownership matter most?

Then share power there. This might look like:

- Co-designing priorities
- Inviting dissent early (before decisions are final)
- Letting teams shape *how* goals are met
- Trusting professionals to adapt intelligently within a clear frame

Wise leaders don't share power everywhere. They share it strategically.

### 3. Respond to Mistakes as Information, Not Insubordination

Nothing reveals your leadership stance faster than how you respond when things go wrong.

**Control-driven responses sound like:**

- "Why didn't you follow the plan?"

- "Who approved this?"
- "This can't happen again."

**Trust-driven responses sound like:**

- "What were you seeing at the time?"
- "What can we learn from this?"
- "What do we need to adjust moving forward?"

If mistakes are punished, agency disappears. If mistakes are examined, learning expands.

## 4. Let Go of Being the Smartest Person in the Room

This is one of the hardest—and most liberating—shifts for leaders. Agency doesn't require leaders to have all the answers. It requires leaders to *make room for others' thinking*.

Ask:

- "What am I missing?"
- "Who sees this differently?"
- "What would improve this from your perspective?"
- "What would you recommend?"

When leaders model curiosity instead of certainty, trust grows. People stop performing for approval. They start contributing authentically.

## 5. Protect the Culture You're Trying to Build

Trust is fragile in systems designed for control.

Leaders must actively protect:

- Time for thinking
- Space for dialogue
- Psychological safety

- Shared ownership

This means:

- Challenging performative compliance
- Naming misalignment when you see it
- Interrupting fear-based practices—even when they're familiar
- Modeling vulnerability and learning publicly

**Culture doesn't change because you say the right thing. It changes because you consistently do the trusting thing.**

## What This Might Look Like in Practice

### In a School

**The situation:**

A principal used to approve every instructional decision: lesson plans, assessment choices, grouping strategies, even classroom library book selections. Teachers waited for permission before trying anything new. Innovation stalled. Teachers felt micromanaged.

**The shift:**

The principal called a staff meeting and said: "Here's what's non-negotiable: our shared learning priorities and our commitment to equity. Beyond that, I trust you to make instructional decisions that serve your students. You're the experts in your classrooms."

She clarified her role: "I'm here to support, resource, and remove obstacles—not to approve every choice. Let's figure this out together."

Then she invited grade-level teams to co-design assessment approaches within the non-negotiables.

**The result:**

Teacher leadership exploded. Teams started piloting new strategies, sharing what worked, and refining practice collaboratively. Student learning improved because teachers were finally free to respond to what students actually needed.

The principal's role shifted from bottleneck to capacity-builder. She told me later: "I was exhausted trying to control everything. Now I'm energized watching what they create."

## In a District or Network

**The situation:**

A network of charter schools operated through compliance monitoring. District leaders visited schools with checklists, looking for "fidelity to the model." Principals felt scrutinized, not supported. Innovation was rare because risk felt dangerous.

**The shift:**

New leadership shifted the approach entirely. Instead of compliance visits, they created:

- **Inquiry cycles:** Schools identified their own questions and challenges
- **Peer learning networks:** Principals learned from each other instead of being evaluated against each other
- **Transparent data sharing:** All schools saw everyone's data—not to rank, but to learn
- **Permission to pilot:** Schools could experiment with new approaches as long as they tracked impact and shared learning

The message shifted from *"Are you doing it right?"* to *"What are you learning, and how can we support you?"*

**The result:**

Innovation spread rapidly across the network. Schools took thoughtful risks because failure was reframed as learning. One principal said: "I feel like a professional again—not someone being watched for compliance."

Student outcomes improved because schools were solving real problems, not just performing compliance.

## In a Nonprofit Organization

**The situation:**

In a youth development nonprofit, the executive director and board made all major decisions about programs, partnerships, and resource allocation. Frontline staff—the people actually working with young people daily—executed plans but had no voice in shaping them. Programs felt disconnected from community needs. Staff turnover was high.

**The shift:**

The new executive director restructured decision-making:

- **Program design teams:** Frontline staff co-designed new initiatives alongside leadership
- **Community feedback loops:** Young people and families informed program direction through regular listening sessions
- **Budget transparency:** Staff saw the full budget and understood constraints
- **Shared decision protocols:** Major decisions required input from people closest to the work

One specific change: Before launching a new mentorship program, the director asked frontline staff, "You work with these young people every day. What do they actually need? What would make this program meaningful—not just fundable?"

**The result:**

Staff retention increased dramatically. One team member said: "They asked what we were seeing on the ground—and then actually built that into the program. That's never happened before, and it lets me know my expertise matters. I'm not just a pair of hands; I'm a thinking partner."

Program quality improved because designs reflected real community needs, not assumptions from a boardroom. Young people noticed the difference too.

## In a Corporate Organization

**The situation:**

A software company operated top-down. Executives created roadmaps and strategic priorities. Product teams waited for directives about what to build next. Teams had expertise but no autonomy. Motivation was low. Good people were leaving.

**The shift:**

The new VP of Product made a bold move. She said to teams: "Here's what we're accountable for as a company: revenue targets, customer retention, and strategic positioning. Here's the timeline we're working within. Beyond that—how we get there, what we prioritize, how we solve problems—that's yours to figure out."

She created:

- **Team autonomy within boundaries:** Each team owned their domain and could make decisions without executive approval

- **Transparent constraints:** Everyone understood the "why" behind business goals
- **Bi-weekly showcases:** Teams shared progress, challenges, and learning with each other—not for approval, but for collective problem-solving
- **"Stop doing" permissions:** Teams could abandon initiatives that weren't working, without penalty

**The result:**

Decision velocity increased dramatically. One product manager said: "We ship features in weeks that used to take months—because we're not waiting for five layers of approval."

Accountability actually strengthened because ownership was real. Teams cared about outcomes because they shaped the path to get there. Employee satisfaction scores rose. Attrition dropped.

The VP told me: "I thought letting go of control would be terrifying. It's been liberating—for all of us."

## Common Pitfalls (And How to Avoid Them)

### 1. Confusing Trust with Absence

Leaders still matter—deeply. Trusting people doesn't mean stepping back from the work. It means showing up differently—as a supporter and obstacle-remover rather than an approver and controller.

**What to try instead:** Stay present. Provide support. Remove obstacles. Coach. Just don't micromanage.

### 2. Sharing Power Without Clarity

That feels like abandonment, not trust. When people are given ownership without understanding the boundaries, the non-negotiables, or the purpose behind the work, they don't feel empowered—they feel exposed. Clarity isn't the opposite of trust. It's what makes trust feel safe.

**What to try instead:** Be transparent about what's fixed and what's flexible. Give clear boundaries.

### 3. Expecting Trust Without Modeling It

People notice inconsistencies immediately. If you say you want people to take risks but respond to mistakes with blame, the message received is clear: the invitation wasn't real. Trust has to be demonstrated before it will be returned.

**What to try instead:** Trust first. Model vulnerability. Admit when you don't know.

### 4. Retreating to Control Under Pressure

This is when trust is most tested—and most needed. Under pressure, the instinct to centralize control is powerful and understandable. But retreating to control in a crisis teaches people that trust was always conditional.

**What to try instead:** When pressure rises, resist the urge to grip tighter. Slow down. Involve others.

### 5. Assuming Trust is Soft

It's one of the hardest leadership disciplines there is. Holding boundaries while distributing power, staying present without micromanaging, maintaining confidence in people even when things wobble—none of that is soft.

**What to try instead:** Recognize that trust requires courage, clarity, and consistency. Treat it with the same seriousness you'd give any other high-stakes leadership skill.

## Tiny Shift: Try This Tomorrow

In your next leadership moment—formal or informal—try this:

**Name the goal.**

**Name the constraint.**
**Then ask: "How might you approach this?"**

Listen. Resist fixing. Notice what happens.
That moment—small as it is—is leadership through trust.

## Reflection Prompts

1. Where do you default to control—and why? What are you protecting?
2. What fears surface when you imagine sharing power more openly?
3. Where have you seen trust unlock capability in others?
4. How do people experience your leadership under pressure? What might your response to mistakes teach them?
5. What could it look like to lead as if agency were not a risk—but the goal?

## Closing Note

Across this final section, one truth becomes clear: **Agency is not a program, a strategy, or a personality trait. It is the result of leadership choices—made daily—about trust, time, voice, and power.**

When leaders protect conditions instead of micromanaging behavior, people don't disengage. They step forward. They think more deeply. They take responsibility that lasts.

**Leading for agency isn't about letting go of leadership. It's about redefining it**—so growth, learning, and contribution are no longer dependent on one person at the top, but are woven into the fabric of the whole system.

That is leadership that lasts.

# AFTERWORD

## WHAT COMES NEXT

If you're holding this book at the end of a long week, you're probably carrying a lot. People. Decisions. Expectations. Unfinished conversations. Things you wish had gone differently. Things you're proud of. Things you're still figuring out.

Whether you work with children or adults—or both—you're likely doing work that matters deeply and resists easy answers. You're navigating systems that ask for certainty while living in realities that demand responsiveness. You're balancing care and accountability, urgency and patience, structure and freedom.

In that tension, it's easy to grip tighter. To add another strategy. To clarify one more expectation. To fix just one more thing yourself. Not because you don't trust others. Because the stakes feel high. And because you care.

This book was never an argument for caring less. It's an invitation to care ***differently.***

Over these chapters, we've returned again and again to a simple but challenging idea:

---

**Agency doesn't come from doing more. It comes from designing conditions where people can think, choose, contribute, and grow —together.**

---

That work is subtle, often invisible, and deeply countercultural.

## What's Different Now

If this book has done its work, you're noticing things you couldn't see before.

**You're noticing the web, not just the ladder.**

Where you used to see individuals succeeding or struggling alone, you now see the relationships, routines, and structures that either support or undermine their capacity to contribute.

**You're noticing compliance masquerading as engagement.**

Where you used to see quiet, productive-looking rooms and assume learning was happening, you now ask: "*Whose thinking is actually at work here?*"

**You're noticing what you measure—and what you're missing.**

Where you used to trust the data at face value, you now ask: *"Are we measuring what actually matters? Or just what's easy to count?"*

**You're noticing when you're doing the thinking for people instead of with them.**

Where you used to design finished plans and wonder why people weren't more invested, you now see the invisible choices you could share.

**You're noticing the difference between speed and depth.**

Where you used to equate coverage with progress, you now recognize when slowing down would actually accelerate learning.

**You're noticing strengths, not just gaps.**

Where you used to scan for what's missing or broken, you now look for what's already working—and how to build from there.

---

**Agency grows inside clarity. And now, you see more clearly.**

---

## What You Might Stop Doing Tomorrow

Noticing is the first step. But agency requires action—or sometimes, strategic inaction.

Here's what you might release:

- **Stop filling every silence.** Let questions breathe. Let thinking catch up. Trust the pause.
- **Stop designing alone.** Invite the people closest to the work into shaping it—even if it's messier and slower at first.
- **Stop confusing urgency with importance.** Protect time for what matters. Say "not now" to what doesn't.
- **Stop starting with what's wrong.** Lead with capability. Name strengths. Build from there.
- **Stop adding without subtracting.** Every new priority requires releasing an old one. Be honest about trade-offs.
- **Stop trying to be the answer.** Be the question. Be the structure. Be the listener. Let others do more of the thinking.

---

**Agency isn't about doing more. It's about designing better.** And now, you have the lens to see where that design work matters most.

---

## The Resistance You'll Face

Let's be honest about what happens when you start shifting from control toward agency.

Some people will resist—not because they're difficult or unmotivated, but because the shift asks something of them they're not used to giving: their thinking, their uncertainty, their willingness to co-create rather than comply.

Some systems will push back. Structures designed for compliance don't easily accommodate shared design. Timelines built for efficiency don't naturally make space for dialogue. Metrics focused on counting don't easily capture growth.

And some days, you'll resist too. Because control is familiar. It's faster in the short term. It feels safer when stakes are high.

This is normal. Expected. Human.

The question is not whether resistance will show up. The question is: *what will you do when it does?*

## The Shift That Changes Everything

Here's what I've learned after years of working in learning spaces, boardrooms, coaching conversations, and leadership teams around the world:

---

The future does not belong to the loudest leaders or the most tightly managed systems. **It belongs to the environments that know how to cultivate ownership.**

---

In a world that defaults to control, choosing agency is not soft. It is strategic. It restores energy. It builds trust. It increases contribution. It makes work sustainable. And it reminds people of something they have had all along: the capacity to think, to choose, to shape, to grow.

But here's the thing about agency: you can't demand it. You can only design for it.

## What to Do Tomorrow

If you take nothing else from this book, take this: ***Start small.***

You don't have to redesign everything. You don't need to change your entire system. You don't need to overhaul your curriculum or restructure your organization. You just need to notice one place where you're holding control that might be better shared.

> One meeting where you could invite thinking instead of delivering answers.
>
> One decision where you could design with people instead of for them.
>
> One moment where you could pause and ask: *"Whose thinking is doing the heavy lifting right now? And is that the thinking I want to grow?"*

That's enough. ***Because tiny shifts compound.*** One conversation leads to another. One small success builds confidence for a bigger risk. One person feeling genuinely heard begins to trust that their voice matters—and starts using it more often.

And slowly—sometimes maddeningly slowly—the culture shifts. Not because you implemented a program. But because you designed differently.

## A Final Invitation

This book ends where all meaningful work begins: ***with a choice.***

You can continue designing systems that depend on control—managing behavior, monitoring compliance, carrying the thinking for others. Or you can design systems that cultivate agency—building clarity, inviting contribution, sharing power where it matters most.

Both are hard. But only one is sustainable. Only one restores energy instead of depleting it. Only one builds the capacity people will need to navigate the complexity ahead.

---

So as you return to your classroom, your team, your organization, your community, consider this question—not as a test, but as a companion:

---

**What might become possible if I held on tightly to just a little bit less?**

---

Less control. Less certainty. Less doing for others what they could learn to do with one another.

And in that released space … More thinking. More trust. More shared ownership. More humanity.

That's not the end of the work. ***It's a way into it.***

Here's to the courage it takes to try something new, the grace we need when it doesn't go perfectly, and the communities that sustain us through it all. May we all have the wisdom to know what's worth holding tightly—and the courage to release what isn't.

That's where agency begins.

Tiny shifts. Shared design. Lasting growth.

♡ Tonya

# APPENDIX

The chapters offered frameworks and moves. The appendix offers pathways and language.

Here you'll find:

- **The Agency Pathways Index: A Starting Point, Not a Sequence** with ways to navigate this book based on your role and context
- **A Shared Language for Agency: Key Terms and Concepts** with definitions for the ideas used throughout the book.
- **Where These Ideas Come From: The Thinkers Behind the Frameworks** with the researchers and frameworks that shaped this work.

Think of this section as a companion—something to return to when you need direction, want to go deeper, or are curious about the thinking behind the thinking.

Use what serves you. Skip what doesn't. Return to what helps.

# THE AGENCY PATHWAYS INDEX

## A STARTING POINT, NOT A SEQUENCE

You don't need to read this book from front to back.

You can start where your work—and your energy—most need support right now.

Use the pathways below to jump into the chapters and ***tiny shifts*** most likely to meet you where you are.

## IF YOU ARE A CLASSROOM TEACHER

... and you want to move beyond compliance toward real engagement and ownership, consider:

- **Reframe engagement as thinking, not behavior** → *Mistaking Compliance for Engagement* (Ch. 2)
- **Co-construct direction so students can self-direct** → *The Power of Shared Direction* (Ch. 5)
- **Design lessons with students, not just for them** → *Design with People, Not for Them* (Ch. 6)
- **Use routines to make choice feel safe, not risky** → *Build Routines That Make Choice Safe* (Ch. 7)

- **Make thinking visible without adding more work** → *Make Thinking Visible* (Ch. 9)

## IF YOU ARE A SCHOOL, DISTRICT, OR ORGANIZATIONAL LEADER

... and you feel like you're carrying too much of the thinking and decision-making, consider:

- **Shift from control to shared responsibility** → *Agency Isn't Independence—It's Interdependence* (Ch. 1)
- **Clarify purpose so people don't wait for permission** → *The Power of Shared Direction* (Ch. 5)
- **Protect time, energy, and focus for what matters most** → *Protecting Time, Energy, and Focus* (Ch. 12)
- **Design feedback that grows people, not pressure** → *Feedback That Grows People, Not Pressure* (Ch. 13)
- **Lead through trust, not micromanagement** → *Leading Through Trust, Not Control* (Ch. 15)

## IF YOU ARE A COACH, FACILITATOR, OR INSTRUCTIONAL LEADER

... and you want to move from "fixing" to partnering in thinking, consider:

- **Ask fewer, better questions** → *Ask Better Questions (and Fewer of Them)* (Ch. 8)
- **Use positive presuppositions to grow confidence and capacity** → *Strength-Spotting as a Daily Practice* (Ch. 11)
- **Design conversations that feed forward, not just back** → *Feedback That Grows People, Not Pressure* (Ch. 13)
- **Build learning communities that sustain growth** → *Building Communities of Practice* (Ch. 14)

## IF YOU WORK IN CORPORATE, NONPROFIT, OR L&D CONTEXTS

… and you want teams who take initiative rather than wait for direction:

- **Design work that people can actually own** → *Design with People, Not for Them* (Ch. 6)
- **Create psychological safety through predictable routines** → *Build Routines That Make Choice Safe* (Ch. 7)
- **Make learning and problem-solving visible across teams** → *Make Thinking Visible* (Ch. 9)
- **Slow down to improve execution and learning transfer** → *Slow Down to Speed Up* (Ch. 10)
- **Replace control with trust—without losing clarity** → *Leading Through Trust, Not Control* (Ch. 15)

## IF YOU ARE AN INDIVIDUAL CONTRIBUTOR

… and you want to reclaim your own sense of agency at work or in learning, consider:

- **Reexamine beliefs that keep you waiting for permission** → *Part I: The Belief Shifts* (Chapters 1-5)
- **Notice where routines either support or restrict your voice** → *Build Routines That Make Choice Safe* (Ch. 7)
- **Use strength-spotting as a way to grow confidence and direction** → *Strength-Spotting as a Daily Practice* (Ch. 11)
- **Find agency through interdependence, not isolation** → *Agency Isn't Independence—It's Interdependence* (Ch. 1)

# A SHARED LANGUAGE FOR AGENCY

## KEY TERMS AND CONCEPTS

The language we use to describe learning, leadership, and change often varies by context. A classroom teacher, a school leader, a corporate L&D professional, and a nonprofit director may use different words to describe the same underlying ideas.

This glossary exists to support shared understanding across sectors. While the jargon may change, the principles of agency remain remarkably consistent. The terms below reflect concepts that appear throughout this book—sometimes in educational language, sometimes in organizational or leadership language—but always grounded in learning.

### AGENCY

Agency refers to the ability to act with intention, choice, and purpose. In learning contexts, agency means learners are not passive recipients of instruction but active participants in making meaning, setting goals, and reflecting on their growth.

Agency is not the absence of structure. It is the presence of meaningful ownership within it.

## ALIGNMENT

Alignment describes the degree to which values, intentions, and practices are working together. In agency-centered systems, alignment supports clarity rather than compliance—helping learners and teams understand *why* certain choices are made.

Alignment is about coherence, not sameness.

## AUTONOMY

Autonomy refers to having meaningful choice within appropriate boundaries. In classrooms and organizations alike, autonomy supports motivation when individuals understand the purpose of the work and have some control over how they engage with it.

Autonomy without support can feel overwhelming; autonomy with clarity builds agency.

## CAPACITY BUILDING

Capacity building is the ongoing development of skills, understanding, and confidence over time. Rather than relying on one-off solutions, capacity building emphasizes sustained growth for individuals and teams.

In this book, capacity building applies equally to students, teachers, and leaders.

## CO-CONSTRUCTION

Co-construction is the practice of building understanding, criteria, or processes together rather than delivering them fully formed. This might include co-creating success criteria, norms, learning goals, or next steps.

Co-construction signals trust and invites ownership.

## COHERENCE

Coherence refers to how well different practices, initiatives, and expectations fit together. High coherence reduces fragmentation and cognitive overload, making it easier to focus on what matters most.

Agency flourishes when systems are coherent enough to be navigable.

## CONSTRAINTS

Constraints are the boundaries within which learning and decision-making occur. In agency-centered environments, constraints are made visible and purposeful rather than hidden or arbitrary.

Well-designed constraints can actually *increase* agency by clarifying what is flexible and what is not.

## DECISION-MAKING AUTHORITY

Decision-making authority refers to who has the power to make which decisions. Making this explicit helps clarify roles and reduces frustration caused by unspoken expectations.

Agency grows when decision-making authority is intentionally shared and clearly communicated.

## ENGAGEMENT

Engagement describes the degree to which learners are cognitively, emotionally, and behaviorally involved in their learning. In this book, engagement is understood as *thinking work,* not compliance or busyness.

Engagement is a result of meaningful learning—not a prerequisite students must earn.

## FEEDBACK

Feedback is information that helps learners understand where they are in relation to a goal and what might support next steps. Effective feedback invites reflection and action rather than simply evaluating performance.

Feedback supports agency when it builds clarity instead of dependence.

## L&D (LEARNING AND DEVELOPMENT)

L&D refers to the corporate function responsible for employee training, professional development, and organizational learning. L&D teams design programs to build skills, support performance, and strengthen culture.

In education, similar work happens through professional learning, coaching, and curriculum design.

## LEARNING INTENTIONS

Learning intentions clarify what learners are working toward and why it matters. They focus attention on understanding rather than task completion.

Clear learning intentions support agency by making learning goals visible and negotiable.

In corporate contexts, these might be called "objectives" or "outcomes."

## METACOGNITION

Metacognition refers to awareness of one's own thinking and learning processes. It includes planning, monitoring, and reflecting on learning.

Agency is strengthened when learners are supported to think about *how* they learn—not just *what* they produce.

## PLC (PROFESSIONAL LEARNING COMMUNITY)

A PLC is a group of educators who meet regularly to collaborate on improving teaching and learning. PLCs focus on shared inquiry, collective problem-solving, and continuous improvement.

In corporate settings, similar structures might be called "communities of practice" or "learning circles."

## PSYCHOLOGICAL SAFETY

Psychological safety is a shared belief that it is safe to take risks, ask questions, and admit uncertainty without fear of embarrassment or punishment.

Psychological safety is a prerequisite for exercising agency—for both young learners and adults.

## SCAFFOLDING

Scaffolding refers to temporary supports that help learners access complex ideas or tasks. These supports are gradually removed as independence increases.

Scaffolding exists to *build* agency, not replace it.

## STAKEHOLDER

A stakeholder is anyone who has an interest in or is affected by a decision, project, or outcome. In education, stakeholders include students, families, teachers, and administrators. In organizations, stakeholders might include employees, clients, partners, and investors.

Recognizing stakeholders helps clarify whose voice and perspective matter in decision-making.

## SUCCESS CRITERIA

Success criteria describe what quality looks like in relation to a learning goal. When co-constructed, they help learners self-monitor and make informed decisions about their work.

Success criteria make expectations transparent rather than implicit.

In corporate contexts, these might be called "performance indicators" or "quality standards."

## SYSTEMS THINKING

Systems thinking involves examining patterns, relationships, and structures rather than focusing only on individual actions. It helps explain why change is often complex and non-linear.

Agency-oriented systems thinking focuses on removing barriers rather than assigning blame.

## VOICE

Voice reflects opportunities for learners and team members to express perspectives, questions, and ideas—and to know those contributions matter.

Voice without influence is symbolic. Voice with impact supports agency.

# WHERE THESE IDEAS COME FROM

## THE THINKERS BEHIND THE FRAMEWORKS

This book did not begin as a theory. It began in classrooms where students were doing everything they were asked—and very little they owned. In leadership meetings where capable people waited for permission before thinking out loud. In organizations full of talented professionals who were exhausted from carrying decisions they were never invited to shape.

Over time, patterns emerged.

Across schools, nonprofits, corporate teams, and leadership spaces, the same conditions kept showing up—sometimes with different language, but with remarkably similar dynamics. Agency flourished when people felt safe enough to think, trusted enough to contribute, and supported enough to grow. It withered when control replaced curiosity, and efficiency crowded out meaning.

The ideas in this book are shaped by that lived work. They are also deeply informed by decades of research across education, psychology, and organizational learning. What follows is not an exhaustive literature review, but a window into the thinking that has quietly informed the Tiny Shifts throughout these chapters.

If you'd like to go deeper, these are good places to begin.

## MOTIVATION, AUTONOMY, AND HUMAN NEEDS

### Pink, D.H. (2009). *Drive: The Surprising Truth About What Motivates Us*. Riverhead Books.

At the heart of agency is a simple truth: people want to have a say in their lives and work.

Daniel Pink's synthesis of motivation research shows that people are most engaged when three conditions are met: **autonomy** (choice over how we work), **mastery** (opportunities to get better at something meaningful), and **purpose** (understanding why the work matters).

These aren't "perks"—they're psychological needs. When systems ignore these needs and rely instead on compliance and external rewards, motivation becomes fragile. When systems design for autonomy, mastery, and purpose, people bring their full selves to the work.

This research underpins many of the ideas in this book, especially the distinction between compliance and agency, and the emphasis on designing environments that make ownership possible rather than demanding it.

### Deci, E. L., & Ryan, R. M. (2000). *Self-Determination Theory*. Guilford Press.

Self-Determination Theory goes even deeper, showing that autonomy, competence, and relatedness are fundamental human needs. When any one of these is missing, people may comply, but they rarely engage deeply. This framework helps explain why "just try harder" messages fail—and why thoughtful design succeeds.

## PSYCHOLOGICAL SAFETY AND THE CONDITIONS FOR LEARNING

Edmondson, A. C. (2018). *The Fearless Organization: Creating Psychological Safety in the Workplace for Learning, Innovation, and Growth*. Wiley.

Agency does not grow in fear.

Amy Edmondson's work on psychological safety helps explain why people stop offering ideas, asking questions, or taking risks when they sense that mistakes will be punished or ignored. Her research—often cited in corporate and organizational contexts—echoes what educators have long known: learning requires safety.

This thinking is woven throughout chapters on feedback, routines, questioning, and leadership. Choice is only meaningful when it feels safe to use.

## LANGUAGE, IDENTITY, AND AGENCY

Johnston, P. H. (2004). *Choice Words: How Our Language Affects Children's Learning*. Stenhouse Publishers.

Johnston, P. H. (2012). *Opening Minds: Using Language to Change Lives*. Stenhouse Publishers.

Peter Johnston's work on the power of language in shaping identity and agency has profoundly influenced this book. His research shows that the words teachers and leaders use—the questions we ask, the feedback we give, the assumptions we convey—have lasting effects on how people see themselves and their capabilities.

Johnston demonstrates that language is never neutral. It either opens possibilities or closes them. It either invites agency or reinforces dependence.

His work on "choice words"—language that assumes competence, invites thinking, and positions learners as capable—appears throughout this book, particularly in chapters on questioning, feedback, and strength-spotting.

When we say "What are you noticing?" instead of "Here's what you should notice," we're using Johnston's insight: that language shapes not just what people learn, but *who they become.*

## GROWTH MINDSET AND IDENTITY FORMATION

### Dweck, C. S. (2006). *Mindset: The New Psychology of Success.* Random House.

Carol Dweck's research on fixed versus growth mindset has fundamentally shaped how educators and leaders think about learning, feedback, and capability.

Dweck's work demonstrates that people's beliefs about whether intelligence and ability are fixed or malleable profoundly affect their willingness to take risks, persist through challenges, and view mistakes as opportunities rather than failures.

When we operate from a fixed mindset, we see ability as static—"I'm either good at this or I'm not." Feedback becomes threatening because it seems to reveal permanent limitations.

When we operate from a growth mindset, we see ability as developable through effort and practice. Feedback becomes useful because it shows us where to grow next.

This distinction matters deeply for agency. When systems praise talent over effort, focus on deficits rather than progress, or treat mistakes as failures rather than learning, they reinforce fixed mindsets—and agency withers.

Dweck's insights inform this book's approach to feedback (Chapter 13), strength-spotting (Chapter 11), and the language we use to position learners as capable.

## LEARNING AS A SOCIAL ACT

### Wenger, E. (1998). *Communities of Practice: Learning, Meaning, and Identity*. Cambridge University Press.

One of the most persistent myths about agency is that it is something individuals develop alone.

Wenger's work challenges that assumption. His research shows that learning is inherently social—that people develop competence, identity, and agency *with* others, not apart from them. Whether we call them classrooms, PLCs, teams, or learning communities, the principle is the same: agency grows through participation.

This perspective informs the book's emphasis on interdependence, shared thinking, and communities of practice across sectors.

## SYSTEMS THINKING AND LEARNING ORGANIZATIONS

### Senge, P. M. (1990). *The Fifth Discipline: The Art & Practice of the Learning Organization*. Doubleday.

When agency struggles, the problem is rarely a lack of motivation. More often, it's the system.

Peter Senge's work on learning organizations helps shift the focus from individual behavior to the structures, routines, and assumptions that shape how people work together. His emphasis on systems thinking aligns closely with the book's attention to routines, pacing, feedback loops, and leadership decisions that either expand or constrain agency.

Agency is not a personality trait—it is a product of design.

## FOCUS, ATTENTION, AND DEEP WORK

Newport, C. (2016). *Deep Work: Rules for Focused Success in a Distracted World*. Grand Central Publishing.

Agency requires more than permission—it requires cognitive capacity.

Cal Newport's research shows that fragmented attention dramatically reduces the quality of thinking and decision-making. When we context-switch constantly, we're busy but not productive. We're moving but not learning.

This work informs the book's chapter on protecting time, energy, and focus—recognizing that meaningful work requires uninterrupted thinking space.

## HIGH-PERFORMING TEAMS AND COLLECTIVE INTELLIGENCE

Duhigg, C. (2016). *Smarter Faster Better: The Secrets of Being Productive in Life and Business*. Random House.

Research on high-performing teams consistently points to a surprising conclusion: outcomes matter less than interactions.

Duhigg's synthesis of research, including Google's Project Aristotle, reinforces the idea that teams thrive when people feel safe to speak, when thinking is shared, and when purpose is clear. These findings echo many of the Tiny Shifts in Part II and Part III—particularly those related to meetings, feedback, and shared decision-making.

## TRUST AND TEAM DYNAMICS

Lencioni, P. (2002). *The Five Dysfunctions of a Team: A Leadership Fable*. Jossey-Bass.

Patrick Lencioni's work on team dysfunction identifies trust as the foundational layer upon which all other dynamics rest. Without trust, teams lose the ability to work through disagreement, commit to shared decisions, hold each other accountable, or stay focused on collective outcomes.

This directly connects to the book's final chapter on leading through trust rather than control—and the recognition that agency cannot exist where trust is absent.

## INTERDEPENDENCE AND COOPERATIVE LEARNING

Johnson, D. W., & Johnson, R. T. (1989). *Cooperation and Competition: Theory and Research*. Interaction Book Company.

Long before "collaboration" became a leadership buzzword, the Johnsons' research demonstrated that structured interdependence leads to deeper learning, stronger relationships, and higher achievement.

Their work supports the book's stance that agency is not about independence alone, but about meaningful contribution within a shared effort.

## FEEDBACK THAT GROWS LEARNING

Hattie, J., & Timperley, H. (2007). "The Power of Feedback." *Review of Educational Research*, 77(1), 81-112.

John Hattie and Helen Timperley's research on feedback has shaped how educators and leaders think about growth. They identify three essential questions feedback must answer:

- **Feed up:** Where am I going?
- **Feed back:** How am I going?
- **Feed forward:** Where to next?

When feedback addresses all three, it becomes a tool for agency rather than evaluation. This framework informs Chapter 13 and appears throughout the book's emphasis on clarity and forward momentum.

## MAKING THINKING VISIBLE

Ritchhart, R., Church, M., & Morrison, K. (2011). *Making Thinking Visible: How to Promote Engagement, Understanding, and Independence for All Learners.* Jossey-Bass.

Ron Ritchhart and his colleagues at Project Zero have spent decades researching what they call "making thinking visible"—the practice of externalizing cognitive processes so they can be examined, shared, and refined.

Their work shows that when thinking becomes visible, learning deepens, misconceptions surface earlier, and students develop metacognitive awareness. This thinking informs Chapter 9 and the book's broader emphasis on designing for cognition, not just behavior.

## COACHING, QUESTIONS, AND THINKING-CENTERED CONVERSATIONS

Costa, A. L., & Garmston, R. J. (2002). *Cognitive Coaching: A Foundation for Renaissance Schools.* Christopher-Gordon Publishers.

Kegan, R., & Lahey, L. L. (2009). *Immunity to Change: How to Overcome It and Unlock the Potential in Yourself and Your Organization.* Harvard Business Press.

Much of the book's emphasis on questions, positive presuppositions, and thinking-centered dialogue is informed by coaching traditions that position growth as a partnership rather than a performance.

Costa and Garmston's work on Cognitive Coaching reinforces the idea that the role of a coach or leader is not to supply answers, but to mediate thinking—through careful listening, intentional questions, and deep respect for the learner's capacity.

Kegan and Lahey's work complements this by showing how well-intentioned people can feel "stuck" not because they lack skill, but because of competing commitments operating beneath the surface. Their research supports the book's focus on curiosity over correction, and trust over control.

Together, these traditions echo a core message of this book: when people feel believed in, they are far more likely to take risks, think deeply, and grow.

## A FINAL NOTE ON RESEARCH AND PRACTICE

Throughout the book, you'll see research ideas woven directly into stories, examples, and Tiny Shifts rather than pulled out into dense citations. That choice is intentional.

This book is not asking you to *implement* research.

It's inviting you to *design differently*—with people, not for them.

If these ideas resonate, the thinkers above offer deeper pathways. If they don't, the invitation remains the same: pay attention to what happens when you shift the conditions, even slightly.

**Agency leaves clues.**

And the best research is the kind you conduct in your own context—noticing what shifts when you slow down, ask better questions, design with others, and lead through trust.

That's where learning lives.

# ACKNOWLEDGMENTS

This book is the product of countless conversations, collaborations, and generous thinking partners over many years. While I can't name everyone who has shaped this work, I want to acknowledge a few key influences and supporters.

To the researchers and thinkers whose work provided the foundation for these ideas—John Hattie and Helen Timperley, Edward Deci, Peter H. Johnston, Ron Ritchhart, Amy Edmondson, Daniel Pink, Carol Dweck, Art Costa and Bob Garmston, and many others—your scholarship made it possible to see patterns I might otherwise have missed. Your rigorous work informed practice, deepened understanding, and made meaningful change possible. Thank you for asking the questions that matter.

To the educators, leaders, and organizations I've had the privilege of working alongside over the past two decades—across international schools, nonprofit organizations, and corporate learning teams spanning six continents—your questions, your struggles, and your commitment to creating better conditions for learning have taught me more than any research ever could. You have been my greatest teachers. This book exists because you trusted me with your challenges, invited me into your thinking, and let me learn alongside you. That trust is a gift I don't take lightly.

To Laura and Evan Robb, who were the first to tell me, "You need to write a book"—and then stayed in my corner cheering me on ever since. Your belief gave me courage when I needed it most.

To Faiza Martin, Elissa Ballard, and Laura McPeak—friends who have walked alongside me through every season of this work. Faiza, during a bleak time when I couldn't see a path forward, you were my lighthouse in the dark. You believed in me, lifted me up, and helped me find the courage to walk away from unhealthy dynamics in order to step into new chapters of my own. Elissa, your listening ear, wise insights, and deep care have carried me through more than you know. And Laura—my best friend since third grade—thank you for being the constant in a life of change, for always being there, and for walking beside me through every new adventure. Thank you all for being the kind of friends who make hard things feel possible.

To those who read early drafts, tested these ideas in their own contexts, and offered invaluable feedback—your insights made this book sharper, clearer, and more grounded in reality. Thank you for your generosity and your honesty.

To my husband, Nathan, who has sat at the laptop with me through late-night writing sessions, idea-testing over dinner, and the inevitable doubts that come with putting your thinking into the world. Thank you for making space for this work and for believing it mattered—even when I wasn't sure.

To my sister, Tabitha, whose love, support, and big-sister protection have made it possible for me to keep moving forward in life. To my mom, Coleen, whose love and excitement for this project have sustained me from across the ocean. And to my cousin, David, and his incredible wife, Carrie—your daily prayers and thoughtful check-ins reminded me I was never alone and that I have gifts worth sharing. Thank you all for being my family.

To my dad, Daniel, who is no longer here to see this book but whose presence lives in every page—your belief that people grow best when given room to think for themselves shaped not just this work, but the person I've become. Thank you for showing me what trust looks like. I hope this honors what you taught me.

To everyone whose name isn't here but whose influence is woven throughout these pages—please know that your thinking, your questions, and your example have shaped this work in ways both visible and invisible. Every conversation mattered. Every challenge you shared taught me something. Every moment of shared discovery lives in these pages. This book belongs to all of us. Thank you.

And finally, I am grateful to God—for the gift of this work, for the strength to complete it, and for the grace that makes both the labor and the rest meaningful. Apart from You, I can do nothing. With You, all things become possible.

♡ Tonya

# ABOUT THE AUTHOR

**Tonya Gilchrist** is an international learning strategist who works alongside educators, leaders, and organizations around the world to design environments where people can think deeply, act with intention, and grow with agency.

Over the past two decades, Tonya has partnered with schools, nonprofits, and leadership teams across diverse cultural and organizational contexts. While the settings and jargon often change, she has noticed a consistent pattern: people are frequently asked to take ownership of work they had little voice in shaping. This book grew out of that observation—and from years of listening closely to the questions, tensions, and quiet frustrations that surface when agency is valued in theory but constrained in practice.

Tonya's work focuses on small, deliberate shifts in belief, design, and leadership that make agency possible—not as independence or abandonment, but as a shared, supported way of working. She is known for bridging research and practice, helping teams move beyond compliance-driven structures toward clarity, trust, and interdependence.

At the heart of her approach is a simple conviction: meaningful learning and leadership are not things we deliver to others. They are things we build together, one thoughtful decision at a time.

# BRING THIS WORK TO YOUR ORGANIZATION

If the ideas in this book resonate, there are several ways we can work together to bring them into your context.

## KEYNOTES & WORKSHOPS

I design keynotes and workshops for leadership teams, conferences, and professional learning communities—across education, nonprofit, and corporate sectors.

Sessions are customized to your context and can range from 60-minute keynotes to full-day and multi-day immersive experiences.

Recent topics include:

- Designing for Agency: How to Build Ownership Without Abandoning Structure
- From Compliance to Commitment: Leading Through Trust, Not Control
- The Transfer Equation: Making Learning Stick in Your Organization

## LEADERSHIP COACHING & CONSULTING

I partner with leadership teams to design systems, routines, and practices that cultivate agency—not as an initiative, but as a way of working.

This work can include:

- Designing with teams (not for them)
- Building shared direction and psychological safety
- Creating feedback systems that grow capability
- Protecting time, energy, and focus at scale

## BULK BOOK ORDERS

Bulk orders (10+ books) are available with discounted pricing for teams and organizations.

Many clients pair bulk book orders with workshops or keynotes for deeper implementation.

Learn more at: tonyagilchrist.com/bulk-orders

## LET'S TALK

If you're curious about what might work for your team or organization, let's start a conversation.

Email: tonya@tonyagilchrist.com
Website: https://www.tonyagilchrist.com/work-with-me
LinkedIn: https://www.linkedin.com/in/tonyagilchrist/

I'd love to hear what you're working on—and explore how these ideas might serve your context.

And if you try one of the tiny shifts in this book, I'd genuinely love to hear about it. Share what you're noticing on LinkedIn (tag me: @tonyagilchrist) or use #TinyShifts so others doing this work can find each other. The best learning from this book won't happen in isolation. It never does.

Printed in Dunstable, United Kingdom

81758470R00143